Calming Student Stress

Calming
Student Stress

Mindfulness, Meditation, and Other Strategies to Reduce Anxiety and Enhance Learning in K–12 Classrooms

Steve Haberlin

ROWMAN & LITTLEFIELD
Lanham • Boulder • New York • London

Published by Rowman & Littlefield
An imprint of The Rowman & Littlefield Publishing Group, Inc.
4501 Forbes Boulevard, Suite 200, Lanham, Maryland 20706
www.rowman.com

86-90 Paul Street, London EC2A 4NE, United Kingdom

British Library Cataloguing in Publication Information Available

Library of Congress Cataloging-in-Publication Data

Names: Haberlin, Steve, 1972– author.
Title: Calming student stress : mindfulness, meditation, and other strategies to reduce
   anxiety and enhance learning in K–12 classrooms / Steve Haberlin.
Description: Lanham, Maryland : Rowman & Littlefield, 2024. | Includes bibliographical
   references. | Summary: "Calming Student Stress is a synthesis of empirical-based
   mind-body practices that have been shown to reduce stress and anxiety, help students
   remain centered and focus, and connect with the learning and each other"—Provided
   by publisher.
Identifiers: LCCN 2024015621 (print) | LCCN 2024015622 (ebook) | ISBN
   9781475873009 (cloth) | ISBN 9781475873016 (paperback) | ISBN
   9781475873023 (epub)
Subjects: LCSH: Classroom environment—Psychological aspects. | Teacher-student
   relationships—Psychological aspects. | Stress in children. | Stress in adolescence. |
   Stress management for children. | Stress management for teenagers. | Mindfulness
   (Psychology)
Classification: LCC LB3013 .H3145 2024 (print) | LCC LB3013 (ebook) | DDC
   372.17/13—dc23/eng/20240521
LC record available at https://lccn.loc.gov/2024015621
LC ebook record available at https://lccn.loc.gov/2024015622

∞™ The paper used in this publication meets the minimum requirements of American
National Standard for Information Sciences—Permanence of Paper for Printed Library
Materials, ANSI/NISO Z39.48-1992.

Contents

Foreword   vii

Preface   ix

Acknowledgments   xi

Chapter 1: Student Stress: The Nemesis of the Classroom   1

Chapter 2: Understanding Stress, the Amygdala, and
    Its Impact on Learning   11

Chapter 3: Getting Parents and School Administration Behind Your
    Cause   21

Chapter 4: Assessing Students' Stress Levels and Helping Students
    Reframe Stress   25

Chapter 5: Mindful-izing the Classroom   31

Chapter 6: Just Breathe! Breathwork Strategies for K–12 Students   43

Chapter 7: Let's Get Moving! Movement-Based Strategies for
    Students   53

Chapter 8: The Vagus Nerve?   75

Chapter 9: Relaxation and Visualization-Based Strategies for the
    K–12 Classroom   83

Chapter 10: Reducing Your Own Stress as an Educator   93

Author's Note   101

Resources   103

References   107

About the Author   123

Foreword

As a teacher of elementary students during the years following the devastating events of 9/11, I searched for ideas to address the emotional needs of my students who were struggling to deal with the unfolding of world events beyond their comprehension or control. During this time, I came across a book of creative visualization strategies for children and was curious as to whether use of these strategies in the classroom might help my students envision a better world and help them to feel more empowered for the future. Because this was a time when teachers were still able to close the door and use their judgment on what was best for their students, I guided my students through the initial exercises, naïvely thinking we might be making some progress. Imagine my consternation when my assistant principal noticed the book on the shelf under the whiteboard and pronounced that such "mumbo-jumbo" had no place within the classroom. Because I had no research to support use of the strategies nor a systematic plan to sell my administrators or parents on the implementation of the non-traditional ideas, I had to abandon my efforts.

Fast-forward to 2006 when I was a newly appointed district administrator in the nation's seventh-largest school district and experienced the physical and emotional effects of the stresses associated with juggling my job along with my responsibilities as a single parent of two high school daughters and the rigorous demands of a doctoral program. When I realized that exercise alone was not enough to help me deal with my life stresses, I decided to add yoga to the mix. I was fortunate that the studio I selected had well-trained instructors in not just the physical practice of yoga, but also in breathwork and meditation. I wasn't able to eliminate the external stresses, but I learned to moderate my anxieties through calling upon breathing techniques, meditation, and visualization. To this day, I credit the discovery and intentional regular practice of yoga as part of a balanced wellness regime to my positive well-being.

The pandemic of 2020 revealed to educators and parents the shortcomings of an education system narrowly focused on academic achievement. If our goal is to empower young people to optimistically create a better future, we must look beyond academic subjects and arm them with strategies and techniques to take charge of their own well-being.

This book provides the science to support the teaching of wellness techniques in today's schools, strategies to garner support from administrators and parents for implementing wellness programs within the classroom, and specific yoga and breathwork exercises appropriate for students of all ages. The time is now for embracing these ideas and empowering the youth of today as they lead us into the future.

Lauri B. Kirsch
Immediate Past-President,
National Association for Gifted Children

Preface

My first year as a teacher was incredibly stressful. I "fell" into teaching middle school after spending time as a newspaper reporter covering the education beat in Central Florida. At the risk of sounding cliché, I felt an urge, a calling to go into education and teach. I didn't attend a formal teacher preparation program but rather got into teaching through a state alternative certificate program, which allowed me three years to become officially certified while working on the job. Well, middle school students don't care that you lack formal training or know how to manage a classroom. There's no grace given. I struggled, but through the help of mentors and learning from my experience, I eventually gained competence and later successfully taught gifted students in elementary classrooms.

While working on my master's degree, I collaborated with a professor at a nearby university on research involving how my students might benefit from practicing various mindfulness-based techniques, including breath meditation and yoga. While mindfulness hadn't quite taken off in schools, most parents of the students agreed to the study. I will never forget how one student—let's call him "Bob"—responded to the intervention. Normally, Bob, a highly gifted and talkative child, struggled to pay attention in class and at times, fell asleep (the result of playing video games well into the night). He was often restless and irritable. However, after practicing mindfulness meditation, he seemed more relaxed, even serene. His restlessness and agitation disappeared, at least for the short-term. Following another activity, where the students practiced mindful eating by fully immersing themselves in tasting food, Bob, diagnosed with attention deficit disorder, exclaimed "I felt like I had one thousand marshmallows in my mouth!"

These kinds of experiences motivated me to continue studying and teaching about mindfulness and meditation practices in education. My own dissertation research involved practicing mindfulness techniques to help me supervise student teachers in a preparation program, and my classroom teaching with undergraduates often involved encouraging them to embed mindfulness-based strategies to help their students.

Let's face it. Schools today can be incredibly stressful places. School leaders are stressed by the constant pressures and changes coming from above. Teachers are stressed with the never-ending expectations and demands placed on them. And students are stressed from academic pressures but also "new" societal pressures coming from social media and information overload. We know that stress (the negative kind) is not conducive to learning and creating positive, supportive classroom environments. Students cannot receive content and master it when they are overly stressed. The information doesn't get in. It simply doesn't stick. Educators now require additional tools and strategies to assist students in self-regulation, stress management, and attentional control.

Mindfulness, yoga, meditation, and deep breathing are tools (what I am calling in this book "mind–body practices") that can assist with this massive challenge. These are not the only tools, but empirical evidence shows they are promising tools. With education and practice, these mind–body practices can be embedded in existing school structures and schedules. In the process, classrooms can become less-stressful places, and students can learn to manage themselves with more skill, which will equip them for more successful, fulfilling lives. I wrote this book to help educators. I *sincerely* want to do what I can to help teachers and others working with students. I know how difficult the job can be, but I also know how important it is. Teachers are incredibly busy people and don't have the time to research and synthesize all the different mind–body practices for stress reduction. I have done that for you in this book. Read through each chapter, paying attention to what resonates. Take what works, what seems to make sense with your classroom, and try it. Stack each strategy on top of another, building a culture and climate of calm and focus—peace even. I wish you all the best!

With peace and gratitude,
Steve Haberlin, PhD

Acknowledgments

I would like to sincerely thank and acknowledge all of the K–12 educators, teachers, counselors, principals, assistant principals, and staff that work with students every day. While the field of education may not always feel supported, you truly do such important and meaningful work. I hope this book helps that cause.

I would also like to express gratitude to the students, families, and parents who helped with the photographs in this book. I could not do it without you.

Finally, this book goes out to all the "contemplative educators," and those who constantly push for holistic education that addresses the "whole person."

Chapter 1

Student Stress

The Nemesis of the Classroom

Michael Bonner, a renowned educator, who works at the Ron Clark Academy in Atlanta, Georgia, a model school that trains teachers worldwide, has his students line up outside the door, a regular routine in his classroom. Loud rap music is booming from speakers on a stage, which is where he stands when he teaches. The students wait with anticipation like they are entering a sporting event or concert. You can see it on their faces; they actually look happy to come to class. Bonner sets a timer (30 seconds), and students begin scurrying to their seats, climbing over some tables, and navigating around one another.

Once the students are in their seats, Bonner "works the crowd," high-fiving students, smiling, and paying compliments. The music continues in the background, a rhythmic beat, as he begins to teach the reading lesson for the day. He turns to the teachers, who have come from all over the country to observe his classroom, and says, "It's all about bringing down the amygdala."

THE AMYGDALA AND YOUR CLASSROOM

Understanding the amygdala (pronounced: "uh-MIG-dull-uh"), two small almond-shaped structures on each side of the brain, and its role in the body's stress response, may be one of the most important things that educators can learn when it comes to helping students cope with anxiety and creating calm classrooms where learning is maximized. If stress and anxiety were a sport, say, football, the amygdala would be the quarterback (or the pitcher for you baseball fans). It's a major player in the production of stress and anxiety in everyone, including the students you teach. Why does this matter? *Because stress and anxiety are the biggest enemies of learning and academic performance* (see, e.g., American College Health Association, 2016; Elias et al., 2011; Cassidy & Johnson, 2022; Sahin & Tuna, 2022). Anxiety, for instance,

1

scrambles the brain's ability to process information and commit it to long-term memory. Brain-imaging technology shows that when the amygdala is overactivated, new sensory information cannot be passed through to parts of the brain associated with learning and memory. So when students are stressed out in your classroom, their brains are essentially turning on an affective filter that blocks out the learning of new content, where information cannot get in. Chronic stress, or repeated, intense exposure to the body's stress response, can literally break down the brain's ability to function and have a shrinking effect on the prefrontal cortex, the part of the brain responsible for memory and learning (more about this in Chapter 2). In today's educational environment, having working knowledge (along with practical brain-based strategies, the core of this book) regarding how the amygdala gets triggered is paramount for educators. For parents, knowing how anxiety is created and having practical strategies to share with their children can be a game-changer.

THE PARASYMPATHETIC NERVOUS SYSTEM AND YOUR CLASSROOM

Perhaps equally important in your quest to create a calming classroom is understanding the autonomic nervous system, including the parasympathetic nervous system's rest and recovery state or relaxation response (Benson & Klipper, 1975). The parasympathetic nervous system is a network of nerves that relaxes your body after periods of danger or stress. This rest and recovery state can be consciously cued through meditation, yoga, deep breathing, and other techniques. Intentionally helping students to activate this state regularly throughout the school day, as a counter to the fight-flight-or-freeze response, which seems not to need much help these days in being triggered, can help transform the learning environment.

STUDENTS ARE MORE STRESSED AND ANXIOUS THAN EVER

In today's classrooms, college and K–12 students appear more stressed than ever (see, e.g., American Psychological Association, 2020; Flannery, 2018; YouthTruth, 2022). The COVID-19 pandemic exacerbated already rising stress and anxiety rates, prompted in part by increased academic pressures to succeed and new societal pressures to fit in coming from social media. Though students have returned to in-person classes, anxiety remains a major concern among educators. For example:

- Health-care providers report higher numbers of behavior issues and aggression, believed to stem from the stress of transitioning from pandemic life back to regular daily routines.
- According to a survey of 220,000 students at 845 schools, "depression, stress, and anxiety is the most prevalent obstacle to learning for secondary students at every grade level, six through twelve" (YouthTruth, 2022, pp. 1–2).
- Depression and suicide rates are on the rise among middle and high school students, with suicide being the second-leading cause of death among those between the ages of fifteen and twenty-four years old (National Alliance on Mental Illness, 2022).

According to the World Health Organization, depression is the leading cause of disability. In addition, "adolescence is an especially vulnerable period for the onset of depression" (Tymofiyeva et al., 2021, p. 1). Anxiety generally precedes depression and is a significant risk factor for teens to develop depression. Nevertheless, while mental health tops the list of barriers to learning among middle and high school students, schools lack the support staff to help them with issues such as depression and anxiety (YouthTruth, 2022). The situation has prompted educators and researchers to collaborate and come up with ways to help students cope with the intensified anxiety, such as a virtual summit held by Education Week in October. There's no question that "effective interventions to improve emotional health and prevent anxiety and depression in adolescents are needed" (Tymofiyeva et al., 2021, p. 1).

Helping Young People Cope with Anxiety

Stress, what is described as the "negative kind," is the nemesis of learning in the classroom. Important note: this book will also address the positive or "upside of stress" (McGonigal, 2015) and help students reframe how they view stress (Chapter 4). But what exactly is "stress"? Stress is generally defined as a physical or mental response to an external event or cause, the body's reaction to pressure, whether it be mental, emotional, or physical. Stress is commonly associated with feelings of being overwhelmed or unable to cope with a situation (National Library of Medicine, 2016). People react differently to stress and potentially stressful events. *Acute stress* is short-term. It goes away after the response. For example, you slam on your brakes in a near accident. Shortly after, you relax, the body returns to homeostasis, and you go on with your day. On the other hand, *chronic stress* can last for weeks, months, or more and result in health problems and the inability to function in daily life.

Anxiety is in the same family as stress, maybe like a cousin. Both involve emotional responses; however, stress is generally caused by an external event or situation. Anxiety is persistent worrying that continues even after the stressor is gone (American Psychological Association, 2022). Anxiety can also produce nearly the same symptoms as stress: difficulty focusing, fatigue, irritability, insomnia, and muscle tension.

Chronic stress or anxiety disorders may require psychotherapy and/or medication, and this book is in no way meant to take the place of medical treatment. Rather the intent is to provide educators and others responsible for young people with an understanding and framework for how anxiety and stress are created and experienced, along with practical tools to help students to practice coping with everyday stressors that can interfere with academics and learning in schools. The idea of this book is to provide you, the reader, with a set of evidence-based strategies that you can implement in your classroom or at home. These strategies are exercises and activities you can do with students that don't take long amounts of time or require major instruction. This book saves you time in the sense that the legwork has been done for you regarding researching and experimenting with various amygdala-calming methods. Your role is to consider which ones might work best regarding your grade level, age, classroom dynamics, and levels of stress among students.

During the past two decades, we have learned much more about anxiety and how the brain works. For example, new technologies like magnetic resonance imaging and positron emission tomography scans have rendered detailed information about how the brain responds in various situations (Pittman & Karle, 2015). This research has revealed that two separate pathways in the brain cause anxiety. One path originates in the *cerebral cortex*, the large gray part of the brain that is responsible for higher-level functioning, including language, thought, reasoning, and decision-making. The other path travels more directly, through the *amygdala*, a cluster of neurons located in the middle of the brain, known as the limbic system, and involved with the emotional processes. The amygdala (generally referred to in the singular) is our ancient "alarm" system, responsible for detecting threats and driving the body's ancient fight-flight-or-freeze response (often called the stress response).

As C. M. Pittman and E. M. Karle (2015) assert, "both pathways play a role in anxiety" (p. 14). Armed with knowledge about the pathways and having a more complete picture of how anxiety and the stress response are triggered, educators and other adults can better understand how to help young people cope with anxiety by providing information and encouraging them to engage in various exercises and practices. So what are some of the ways students can mitigate anxiety produced from either the cortex or amygdala? Each chapter of the book will set the groundwork for various types of practices and approaches and provide specific techniques and examples that can be used in the classroom and at home. Here's an overview of the types of methods that can be used to ward off stress and anxiety:

Mindfulness-Based Practices

Mindfulness, or the quality of present-moment awareness, has been found to be highly beneficial when it comes to dealing with anxiety. Studies suggest that regular practice of mindfulness meditation, for example, even just eight weeks, can reduce activity in the amygdala region and promote emotional regulation by enhancing connectivity between the amygdala and the brain's prefrontal cortex (Doll et al., 2016; Joss et al., 2021; Kral et al., 2018; Taren et al., 2015). Mindfulness programs and practices have become more widespread in U.S. classrooms. In one study (Bauer et al., 2019), middle school students, who received eight weeks of mindfulness training, experienced fewer amygdala-related responses and stronger functional connectivity between the right amygdala and the prefrontal cortex. The results appeared to last after meditation as well.

Breathwork

Deep breathing exercises can also help with stress management, emotional regulation, and taming the amygdala (Jerath et al., 2015; Kulkarni, 2014; Yuliana, 2021). Breathing exercises oxygenate the brain and can counteract the impact of amygdala hijacking (more on this process in the next chapter). Various breathing techniques, such as box breathing, in which one holds the breath and breathes out for a specific amount of time, can assist in reducing stress and anxiety (Chen et al., 2017; Norelli et al., 2020). Breathing-based meditation techniques have been found to help symptoms of post-traumatic stress disorder among military veterans (Seppala et al., 2014). Breathwork has also been reported to help students with test anxiety (Paul et al., 2007).

Movement

Practices that involve moving the body, such as yoga, have also been found to have a positive impact on the amygdala and anxiety, including reduced amygdala activation and improved emotional regulation (Desai et al., 2015; Gothe et al., 2019; Gotink et al., 2018). Combining yoga practice with meditation and breathing exercises seems highly promising as an anxiety-busting intervention. Adolescents who practiced guided meditations, yoga-based movement, and breathing exercises for twelve weeks showed significant reductions in anxiety levels and decreased amygdala activity (Tymofiyeva et al., 2021).

Imagery

The use of imagery, or visualization, has also been recommended as an anxiety-reducing strategy and approach to calming the amygdala (King, 1988; Pile et al., 2021; Pittman & Karle, 2015). Imagery is used as a therapeutic technique, where one uses their imagination to achieve a desired outcome. In the case of anxiety reduction, the idea is that intensely visualizing, for instance, yourself relaxing on the beach or in a peaceful forest, can help an individual achieve the deep breathing and relaxed muscle response needed to reduce activation of the amygdala.

Vagus Nerve

Techniques that stimulate the vagal nerve, the longest nerve that connects the brain with the internal organs and controls the body's parasympathetic nervous system (rest and relaxation), also show promise when it comes to anxiety reduction (George et al., 2008; Rosenberg, 2017). The vagus nerve or *wandering nerve* is responsible for regulating the heartbeat, breathing, and blood pressure and has a major role in telling your muscles when to constrict and relax. Though research remains in the early stages, there has been an intensified focus on vagus nerve therapy research, suggesting that related practices might decrease depression and anxiety, for example (George et al., 2002). Appropriate strategies for students that seem to stimulate this nerve could involve humming, chanting, slow rocking, and belly breathing.

The purpose of this book is to deeply explore all of these possibilities for helping students learn to tame their amygdala and cope with increasing levels of anxiety brought on by society, technology, and education. The remainder of the text will unpack each of these areas, providing guidance on specific methods as well as addressing when and where these strategies might fit into your classroom or school. The following is a preview of what each chapter promises to offer:

CHAPTER 2: UNDERSTANDING STRESS, THE AMYGDALA, AND ITS IMPACT ON LEARNING

In this chapter, we will unpack the role of the brain's amygdala and its relationship to the body's fight/flight/freeze response and cover in depth the two neural pathways leading to the cause of anxiety. With this understanding, you will learn how the amygdala can hijack the brain's prefrontal cortex, thus preventing learning from occurring. Factors such as how the amygdala can be triggered and communicated with other parts of the brain; the impact of diet, exercise, sleep, and thinking on the amygdala; and other topics will be covered. In addition, we will also explore the autonomic nervous system, focusing on the parasympathetic nervous system, which is responsible for the rest and recovery (RR) state, and how understanding how this state is activated can be a game-changer in the classroom. The chapter wraps up by providing a practical framework for implementing the strategies presented in this book.

CHAPTER 3: GETTING PARENTS AND SCHOOL ADMINISTRATION BEHIND YOUR CAUSE

Readers will gain advice on how to communicate and introduce the use of stress-reducing strategies, such as mindfulness and yoga, and handle possible resistance or concerns. Furthermore, specific strategies for getting families on board with sharing these practices will be provided, along with how to gain support from school administrations and the community.

CHAPTER 4: ASSESSING STUDENTS' STRESS LEVELS AND HELPING STUDENTS REFRAME STRESS

Prior to studying the various mind–body classroom strategies, it makes sense to focus on learning about different tools, strategies, and ideas to monitor students' stress levels and well-being on a consistent basis. This will serve as a sort of diagnostic assessment, helping educators decide what and how many stress-reduction methods are needed. This information can also be used after stress-busting strategies are implemented to determine how things are working. The latter part of the chapter will present another significant aspect of this work: helping students reframe the way they think about stress and develop a healthy relationship with stress.

CHAPTER 5: MINDFUL-IZING THE CLASSROOM

This chapter provides you with a comprehensive look at the practice of mindfulness within K–12 settings as well as its impact on the brain, including the amygdala, and the use of mindfulness as an anxiety-coping approach. You will learn specific mindfulness-based, student-friendly strategies that you can implement in your classroom.

CHAPTER 6: JUST BREATHE! BREATHWORK STRATEGIES FOR K–12 STUDENTS

This chapter will begin with sharing research regarding breathwork and anxiety. You will study evidence-based strategies that involve using various breathing techniques to calm the amygdala and deal with triggered responses. Specific, age-appropriate breathing techniques for students and examples will be shared.

CHAPTER 7: LET'S GET MOVING! MOVEMENT-BASED STRATEGIES FOR STUDENTS

We will transition to exploring practices that use movement and the body to reduce anxiety, including yoga, tai chi, and progressive muscle relaxation. Research around this method will be provided as well as specific strategies to introduce to students.

CHAPTER 8: THE VAGUS NERVE?

Background on emerging research on the vagus nerve, our longest nerve responsible for activating the parasympathetic nervous system (rest and recovery), as a major anxiety-reducing component will be covered. From there, specific vagal techniques, such as chanting, movement, and breathing, will be presented within the context of your classroom.

CHAPTER 9: RELAXATION AND VISUALIZATION-BASED STRATEGIES FOR THE K–12 CLASSROOM

This chapter delves into the practices of relaxation methods, namely, Progressive Muscle Relaxation, which has been around since the 1920s, and visualization or mental imagery, a technique used for decades by top-performing athletes and high-achievers. Specific relaxation and mental rehearsal activities, adapted for elementary and secondary students, will be described.

CHAPTER 10: REDUCING YOUR OWN
STRESS AS AN EDUCATOR

Monitoring and managing your own stress and anxiety levels also matters! Therefore, to conclude this work, a summary of research on teacher burnout will be provided along with practical strategies you can employ as an educator to manage and reduce stress and keep yourself calm, energized, and at your best in the classroom.

Chapter 2

Understanding Stress, the Amygdala, and Its Impact on Learning

Everyone is talking about how life in the twenty-first century is more *stressful*. Students and teachers are more stressed than ever. But what exactly is "stress"? The word "stress" is a commonly used word in society but is defined in various ways. The first, most generic definition for stress was proposed by Hans Selye (1976), as a response of the body to any demand. In layman's terms, stress is generally thought of as a feeling of emotional or physical tension (Medline Plus, 2023) or as A. Rushton, 2004, explains, "simply put, anything that makes you anxious, frustrated, unhappy, angry, or tense" (p. 11). A reframed definition of stress, one that helps position stress in a more positive light (more about this later), is from health psychologist, Kelly McGonigal (2015), "Stress is what arises when something you care about is at stake" (p. xxi).

"Good" Stress

Dubbed by the World Health Organization as the "Health Epidemic of the 21st Century," stress has been estimated to cost the United States an estimated $300 billion a year (e.g., medical, legal, insurance costs, lost productivity). A manageable level of stress is normal and healthy. *Positive stress*, or what is known as eustress, characterized by brief increases in heart rate and mild elevations of hormone levels, can increase alertness and performance. *Tolerable stress* involves the activation of the body's alert system more intensely in response to more severe or longer-lasting difficulties, such as the loss of a loved one or a natural disaster. In some cases, stress can provide us with more energy and resilience. For example, one study found that higher levels of DHEA, the "good hormone" produced during the stress response, can predict academic persistence and resilience in college students (Wemm et al., 2010). More recent research supports the idea that it is our mind-set toward stress that might be most important. As McGonigal (2015) asserts, "The latest science reveals that stress can make you smarter, stronger, and more successful. It helps you learn and grow. It can even inspire courage and compassion" (p. xvi).

When Stress Doesn't Serve Us (or Student Learning)

Toxic or *chronic stress* happens when an individual experiences frequent, intense, and/or long-lasting events—the body's fight-flight response is activated for too long. Causes of chronic stress include physical or emotional abuse, exposure to violence, food scarcity, extreme poverty, and substance abuse in the home (University of Oregon, n.d.). Too much stress can wreak havoc on our minds and bodies, causing physical and psychological harm. In fact, stress affects all the body's systems, including the musculoskeletal, respiratory, cardiovascular, endocrine, gastrointestinal, nervous, and reproductive systems (American Psychological Association [APA], 2023).

What's the Difference Between Stress, Anxiety, and Trauma?

There is a fine line between stress and anxiety. As the American Psychological Association (2022) explains, stress is generally caused by an external trigger and can be short- or long-term in nature. On the other hand, anxiety is persistent, excessive worrying that continues even after the external stressor is gone. Both stress and anxiety can produce similar symptoms, including anger, fatigue, muscle pain, irritability, and trouble sleeping. In addition, both mild stress and mild anxiety respond well to the same types of coping mechanisms. Trauma, which has gained interest in education in recent years, can be defined as "an emotional response to a terrible event like an accident, rape, or natural disaster. Immediately after the event, shock and denial are typical. Longer term reactions include unpredictable emotions, flashbacks, strained relationships, and even physical symptoms like headaches or nausea" (APA, 2023). As an educator, it is beneficial to be versed in the mechanics of stress, anxiety, trauma, and anything else that can negatively affect learning and social-emotional development and the establishment of a positive classroom environment.

The Role of the Sympathetic Nervous System

To understand more about stress and anxiety, we need to have some background and understanding of how the nervous system operates. Our nervous system is made up of all the nerve cells in the body, and through this system, we communicate with the outside environment and inside our body. The nervous system allows us to receive information through our senses, process that information, and trigger necessary reactions or responses. For example, if you touch something hot (the stove or a hot plate), our nervous system sends pain signals to the brain and we reflexively pull our hand back (National Library of Medicine, 2016). Our nervous system can be divided into two parts: (1) the central nervous system, which includes the nerves in the brain and spinal cord, and (2) the peripheral nervous system, which contains all the other nerves in the body. Within both these systems, the nervous system can be further defined as whether it is voluntary, controlling things we are consciously aware of such as moving an arm or leg, and involuntary, or controlling bodily processes we are not conscious of, such as breathing or heartbeat. The involuntary system is made up of three parts: the sympathetic, parasympathetic, and enteric or gastrointestinal systems.

Let's look closer at the sympathetic nervous system (SNS), particularly how it relates to the stress response (and how students in your classroom get stressed or triggered). The SNS, sometimes called the "automatic" nervous system, controls our ability to respond to dangerous or stressful situations using what is commonly called the fight-or-flight response (this has been expanded to include "freeze" as a third response). When faced with danger or stress—or *perceived* danger or stress—the SNS is activated, preparing the body for action. The stress response actually occurs in the brain, where distress signals are sent from the amygdala to the hypothalamus (more on these areas of the brain later in this chapter). Adrenal glands begin pumping adrenaline, the hormone epinephrine, into the bloodstream (Harvard Medical School,

2020). Our pupils enlarge to let more light in and help us see better, our heart beats faster to deliver more oxygen to the body, our digestion slows to allow energy to flow to other parts of the body (not a good time to sit and eat when faced with danger), muscles tighten to prepare for battle or running (Cleveland Health Clinic, 2023). The SNS is designed to protect us, an ancient, built-in survival mechanism; however, the stress response can be triggered regularly by situations that are not life-threatening, only *perceived* as a danger or threat. For instance, work demands, traffic jams, or difficult family situations can activate the SNS. Chronic, low-level stress can over-activate the SNS, causing various health problems. Too much adrenaline, for example, can damage blood vessels and arteries, raise blood pressure, and increase the chance of a heart attack or stroke (Harvard Medical School, 2020). Educating K–12 students about how our SNS works and managing the stress response as they progress through life can be life-changing. Allowing the SNS to inform classroom practices and establishing safe, supportive learning environments can greatly serve educators, regardless of the grade level or subject area.

The Role of the Parasympathetic Nervous System

As mentioned above, the parasympathetic nervous system, or PNS, is part of our autonomic nervous system. If the SNS was the high-energy, worked-up brother in the family, the PNS would be his calmer, quieter sibling. The two systems—while seemingly opposite—work together to keep us in balance. The PNS controls the body's ability to relax and helps maintain our resting heart rate (typically 60 to 100 beats per minute) by doing something known as *downregulating.* During daily life, we are constantly faced with stressors (e.g., running late for work, having to give a presentation at work, technology going down during a Zoom call, receiving a call from your child's teacher or principal), which can activate the SNS, causing our muscles to tense, elevating our heart rate, increasing our blood pressure, and dilating the pupils. Even if the stressor is only a perceived threat, our ancient fight-flight-freeze response kicks in, and we experience stress. The PNS's job is to bring us back down, to bring us back to homeostasis through a process called rest and digest, where we experience decreased heart rate and blood pressure, relaxation in the muscles, and deeper breathing—the opposite conditions brought on by the SNS. The PNS operates using a nerve called the vagus nerve (covered in more detail in Chapter 7) to deliver signals from the brain to the body and from the body back to the brain, letting the amygdala know everything is all right.

Want to know if your PNS is working well? A suggested test is to use a heart rate monitor (which can be purchased cheaply online or at your local pharmacy). Inhale deeply, hold it and notice how high your heart rate goes, for instance, 15 to 20 beats per minute. Then, exhale. If your heart rate returns fairly quickly to your resting heart rate, this indicates that your PNS is on point (Long, 2021). Fortunately, there are activities and practices to work your PNS and achieve what is called *vagal tone* or one's resilience to stress and the ability to downregulate. Meditation, mindfulness, yoga, and deep breathing—the practices shared in this book—have been found to help practice and hone the PNS. Teaching students about their nervous system, including how the PNS works and impacts their stress and lives, makes a lot of sense. So does embedding PNS-enhancing practices in the school day.

The Role of the Amygdala

As touched upon in the first chapter, the amygdala is actually a cluster of neurons found in the mid-brain. While small, the amygdala is composed of thousands of circuits of cells that have different purposes (Pittman & Karle, 2015). These various circuits have an influence over love, bonding, sexual behavior, aggression, anger, and fear. The amygdala works by attaching "emotional significance" to situations or objects and to form *emotional memories*" which can be positive or negative (p. 17). This includes attaching anxiety to experiences and creating anxiety-producing memories, and this process is as unconscious as the liver aiding our digestion. It's happening and can have a profound impact on our behaviors and life, but we are unaware. As explained in the section on the SNS, when an individual experiences a stressful event or perceives danger, the amygdala sends a distress signal to the hypothalamus, which functions as a sort of command center, communicating to the rest of the body through the autonomic nervous system (Harvard Medical School, 2020). The SNS is activated and the adrenal glands pump adrenaline into the bloodstream, bringing psychological changes (e.g., increased heart rate, muscle tightening, increased energy through glucose). The amygdala and hypothalamus work so quickly and well together that this process can happen before the brain can visually process what is happening. But it's not over yet. After this first rush of adrenaline, the hypothalamus activates the second part of the stress response, known as the HPA axis, which involves the hypothalamus, the pituitary gland, and the adrenal glands. Relying on a series of hormonal signals, the HPA axis tells the SNS to keep the "gas pedal" pressed down (Harvard Medical School, 2020), and if we perceive something as dangerous, the hormone adrenocorticotropic (ACTH) is released from the pituitary gland, which travels to the adrenal glands, releasing cortisol. Consequently, we remain adrenalized and on high alert until the threat subsides, and cortisol levels drop. The PNS then takes over and lessens the stress response, moving us into a rest and digest state.

Amygdala Hijacking

The frontal lobes are two large areas at the front of the brain (the cerebral cortex). This part of the brain allows us to reason, think, make decisions, and plan (Dixon & Dweck, 2022). This is the cognitive process students utilize when engaging in learning. Unlike the amygdala, the frontal lobes provide us time to consciously respond—they are not automatic. The frontal lobes can assist us by helping to decide how and whether to respond to a stressor. For mild to moderately stressful situations, this part of the brain may override the amygdala, allowing us to remain calm and cool as we handle a situation.

However, in today's fast-paced, information age we are more likely to experience psychological, as opposed to physical, threats, which can activate the amygdala and trigger the stress response. When the amygdala overrides the frontal lobes, disabling our rational thinking process and causing emotions such as aggression, anger, and fear, this has become known as "amygdala hijacking," a term coined by psychologist Daniel Goleman (1995) in his book, *Emotional Intelligence: Why It Can Matter More Than IQ*. For students in your classroom, amygdala hijacking can occur from all kinds of sources. A student is triggered that morning, before school, when his parents get into a heated argument. Another student may feel alienated as she enters the cafeteria or checks a social media post, where students have embarrassed or bullied her. In other cases, a student might experience a stress response waiting for a final exam to be administered or handed back. The list goes on.

THE IMPACT OF STRESS AND ANXIETY ON LEARNING

According to the American College Health Association (2016)[, stress is the *biggest enemy* of academic performance. The correlation between poor academic performance and stress has been well researched (e.g., Blumberg & Flaherty, 1985; Clark & Rieker, 1986; Linn & Zeppa, 1984; Struthers et al., 2000). Chronic stress over time short-circuits the brain's ability to function, shrinking the prefrontal cortex, which houses memory and learning. Brain imaging reveals that when the amygdala (the brain's alarm system and center for fear and anxiety) is overactivated by stress, new sensory information literally cannot pass through various parts of the brain connected with learning. Essentially, when mentally stressed, a student's brain will shut down, filtering out learning and new information. In simple terms, "if students are stressed, the information cannot get in" (Willis, 2006, n.p.).

Researchers have found that learning while stressed can have detrimental effects on memory. A study at the University of California–Irvine (2008) revealed that short-term stress, lasting as little as a few hours, could disrupt brain-cell communication in areas connected with memory in learning. This means that even an argument before class or a student receiving unpleasant news could have difficulty retaining information. Similarly, Schwabe & Wolf (2010) tested how university students memorized lists of words while under stressful conditions (the socially evaluated cold pressor test, which involves participants submerging their right hand in ice-cold water for three minutes). When presented with a list of words to memorize, participants "who learned the words while they were stressed remembered significantly less words compared to participants who learned the words during the control condition" (p. 185).

When students are stressed and/or feeling negative emotions, engagement also drops. A study involving 293 high school students supported that the frequency of positive emotions during classes was associated with higher student engagement while the frequency of negative emotions was connected to lower engagement (Reschly et al., 2008). A classroom learning environment, where high levels of stress prevail, can cause a host of problems. A teacher's stress can also spill over to students, impacting their learning and behaviors. Researchers M. A. Milkie and C. H. Warner (2011), who analyzed data collected from more than ten thousand first graders across the United States, reported that stress in a classroom environment can increase the likelihood of students demonstrating attention problems and difficulty with staying on task as well as increasing the frequency of arguments, fights, classroom disruptions, and impulsivity. Stressful classrooms can also increase the internalizing of problems, such as low self-esteem, anxiety, and loneliness.

When considering the impact of stress and negative energy in the classroom, it becomes clear that learning to help students reduce stress, anxiety, and being triggered is essential to creating conditions for a calm, supportive learning environment. In this age of heightened tensions in schools, becoming educated about the amygdala, the nervous system, and how the mind–body system creates stress is paramount. Possessing an ample, diverse stress-reducing toolbox, full of classroom-friendly strategies, has become an integral part of a teacher's pedagogy.

THE CONTEXT FOR MIND–BODY PRACTICES IN K–12 CLASSROOMS

In her book *Mindfulness and Yoga in Schools: A Guide for Teachers and Practitioners*, C. P. Cook-Cottone (2017) posits a framework to situate how practices such as mindfulness fit into existing movements and education paradigms. To understand this useful conceptual framework, you need to be familiar with three emerging areas. The first is *social-emotional learning* (SEL). There has been a surge in SEL programs across school districts, with the main competencies of SEL centering on helping students develop emotional regulation, self-awareness, and relationship skills. The idea of this movement is that education spans beyond solely preparing students for academics. To become productive, successful citizens, they must also possess social-emotional intelligence. The second component of Cottone's framework is *service learning*, which is "based on the belief students should be involved in their own learning and learning is active, based in experience, and has a

direct connection to caring and community." The final piece in the framework
is contemplative practices, which include mindfulness and yoga. The term,
"contemplation," is derived from the Latin word *contemplare*, which means
to observe or gaze, as in to look at something intently. While various definitions exist for contemplative pedagogy and practices, contemplative practices
within education are those that involve systematically cultivating awareness.
Though mindfulness, yoga, and other practices featured throughout this book
can certainly be categorized as "contemplative," the author has chosen to
use the term "mind–body" practices or "techniques that strengthen the connection between the emotional, mental, and physical aspects of ourselves"
(University of Minnesota, 2023, n.p.).

A Framework for Classroom Mind–Body Practices

Frameworks can serve as mental models or constructs that assist in guiding
the implementation of ideas. They can help our mind order things and see
where to "place" various parts and pieces. Thus, the following framework, the
Classroom Mind–Body Practices Framework (CMBP). The framework provides a practical road map to implement the ideas and strategies in this book.
Make sure to return to this framework after reading through the chapters and
becoming more familiar with mind–body practices.

Table 2.1. Classroom Mind–Body Practices Framework

Things to Consider:	*Things to Implement:*
Assessing Stress Levels: • *What are the current stress levels of your particular students?* • *How would you rate the "stress/tension" of the classroom (1–10)?* • *What might be causing stress in your learning environment?* • *Are there particular students who are more stressed than others?*	• *Keep a "stress" log— observe and document student actions and situations throughout the day* • *Administer an anonymous survey to students asking them about their stress levels* • *Talk with students informally about stress and anxiety (e.g., morning meetings, class meeting)*
Planning for Change: • *What might be some goals/ outcomes for students (e.g., less stress, change in certain behaviors, increase in engagement)?* • *Where could you "find" time to implement a new strategy or change in approach (e.g., during morning meetings, bell work, after lunch, end of day)?* • *What mind–body strategies might be appropriate for students/What might you be interested in implementing?*	• *Make a list of the outcomes you would like to achieve with students* • *List 2–3 "windows" in the school day* • *Write down a mind–body approach you are perhaps familiar with or that resonates (you will learn more about this later in the book)*
Parent Permission/Involvement: • *Who do you need to communicate the plan with? Who are the stakeholders (e.g., parents/students, school administration)?* • *What's the best way to communicate this information?* • *How might you get families/ parents/the community involved in this plan (e.g., back-to-school night, workshop, guest speakers/ instructors)?*	• *Make a list of the people you need to communicate with and in what order* • *Craft an email, a newsletter, a video— whatever works best (note: consider translations for families whose first language is not English)* • *Brainstorm ways to get families and the community involved; perhaps collaborate with other educators who are interested*

(continued)

Table 2.1 *(continued)*

Mind–Body Practices:
- *Consider what stress-reduction strategy or strategies you might like to implement (e.g., mindfulness, breathwork, movement-based visualization).*
- *What might students find most enjoyable, engaging, and relatable?*
- *What strategies most seem to "fit" with your current curriculum and schedule? When might you practice this technique?*
- *Review Chapters 4–8 and learn about the different strategies*
- *Reflect on this question based on your experiences*
- *Look at your daily schedule and note*
- *where a strategy or two might be incorporated*

Follow-Up:
- *Return to the initial parts of this framework: What were students' stress levels and your outcomes? Have you made progress?*
- *What strategies are working to help students reduce stress and focus? What might you revise, enhance, improve, or throw out?*
- *Is it time to implement another strategy? If so, when and where?*
- *Might help to keep a running log or journal. Note any signs of progress*
- *List strategies that might be working. Share these ideas and celebrate with colleagues*
- *Study and read about other mind–body strategies in this book*

Chapter 3

Getting Parents and School Administration Behind Your Cause

Before introducing mind–body methods to reduce stress in the classroom, it is recommended that educators plan how to present these non-traditional approaches to parents, administrators, and other school stakeholders. If you work at a school or district where a mindfulness-based intervention program has been pre-approved and implemented, then your job in experimenting with the ideas in this book will likely be easier. However, if you are pioneering mindfulness, yoga, deep breathing, or other similar practices, there are certain steps you want to take *before* jumping into using the strategies. While mindfulness and other holistic practices have grown in popularity in the United States education system, don't assume that everyone, particularly some parents, will fully embrace your newly found enthusiasm or classroom strategies. In some cases, schools have faced heavy resistance. For example, conservative Christian groups have filed legal action against school districts implementing mindfulness and yoga, arguing that these programs are forms of "stealth" Hinduism or Buddhism, secretly ushering religion into public schools. While respecting diverse beliefs, the purpose of this book is to not justify or argue over whether mindfulness and practices are "secular," but rather to provide a synthesis of researched-based techniques to help students de-stress (for a detailed explanation of this argument, read Brown's [2019] book, *Debating Yoga and Mindfulness in Public Schools: Reforming Secular Education or Reestablishing Religion?*).

GAINING SCHOOL ADMINISTRATION SUPPORT

The first step before incorporating mind–body techniques into the classroom is to discuss your plans with school administration. Schedule a meeting with your school principal and, if possible, the assistant principal, to discuss your interest in incorporating mindfulness, yoga, deep breathing, and strategies to help with the problems of stress and anxiety in the classroom. Cite the research and studies outlined in this book. No need to do extra legwork. This book synthesizes the growing research base around these methods. Present specific benefits that students might gain from practicing these methods, even for short periods, for example, during classroom transitions. Emphasize that instructional time *will not be lost* but rather learning time can be enhanced when students are calmer, more focused, and connected. List a few ideas you plan to try, such as starting each morning meeting with a brief mindfulness moment (Chapter 5) or engaging in deep breathing (Chapter 6) whenever coming back from recess, lunch, or special classes. Finally, assure school administrators that you will clearly communicate these changes to parents and families. Furthermore, seeking out collaborators—teaching colleagues and other educators on campus—can strengthen your cause and give you the added support and confidence needed to gain administration approval. Perhaps first approach a colleague or two who you know are interested in mind–body techniques, or ask around.

GAINING PARENTAL SUPPORT

Your next task is to gain support from parents and families of the students in your classroom. A key to garnering support is to clearly communicate *what* you plan to do as well as *why* you plan to do it. Your ideas can be communicated through a letter or classroom newsletter or through a workshop or meeting. Ideally, presenting these ideas in person (at least initially) during an open house or parent night at the beginning of the school year might be best. During the informational session, the idea is to not only share information about the mind–body strategies but also to include parents in the practices themselves. As Yoga.Ed, which provides program support for school systems, teaches, "If parents experience mindfulness firsthand, it can help eliminate a lot of the misinformation and fear that sometimes stops programs before they can start" (Caleda, 2021, n.p.). You can also provide parents with resources to research, explore, and experiment with the practices at home. Websites such as www.mindfulschools.org/resources/explore-mindful-resources/ offer free videos and information. One idea, from the Center for Educational

Improvement (2021), is for teachers to create short videos of themselves engaged in their favorite mindfulness activities and send it to parents, encouraging them to try it at home with their children.

In addition, share with parents the empirical evidence of engaging in these practices. Share examples of studies where K–12 students have benefited mentally and physically. Focus on the neuroscience findings supporting mindfulness, meditation, yoga, and the other techniques in this book, and as Mindful.org recommends, steer clear of the potentially controversial topic of religion. "One of the most important things we learned from public meetings with parents and the community was to be sure the training is completely secular with no religiosity at all," advises Marilyn Neagley, former director of Talk About Wellness (Gerszberg, 2023, n.p.). Be cognizant of the language you use as an educator, avoiding references to Buddhism or other religious traditions: for instance, not using a commonly used yoga phrase such as *namaste.* School-based interventions have even changed terms such as "yoga" to "mindful movement," or "meditation" to "quiet time" to stress the secular aspect and avoid issues.

Also, plan to communicate options for students whose parents decided against having their children participate in mindfulness, yoga, or related activities. In other words, what will these students do while classmates engage in the mind–body activities? For example, you might inform parents/guardians that students abstaining could read a book of their choice, journal, create art, or participate in some other quiet activity. How will you ensure that these students do not feel "singled out" or excluded from the learning community? This is something to fully consider before revealing your plans to parents and families.

PUTTING IT ALL TOGETHER: PARENT/ ADMIN SUPPORT CHECKLIST

The following checklist was designed to help you plan for gaining parental and school administrative support to introduce mindfulness, yoga, and other non-traditional, mind–body practices in the classroom. Go through the list and make sure you have all the bases covered.

Table 3.1. Parental and School Administration Support Checklist

Action	Completed (with date)
Prepared presentation for school administration (e.g., principal, assistant principal). Compiled relevant research and empirical evidence supporting mind–body practices.Have clear plan for what strategies to use when with students and when they will be implemented.	
Scheduled talk with school administration.	
Secured permission (verbal, preferably written) from school administration and/or school district (if necessary).	
Prepared presentation of mind–body practices in the classroom for parents/families. Determined appropriate delivery mode (e.g., newsletter, letter going home, email, video, open house, parent night). Have gathered necessary research and examples to show how practices can benefit students. Have also considered whether materials need to be translated for languages other than English.	
Notified parents/families of the stress-reduction plan. Have outlined rationale for including mind–body practices but also options for students abstaining from practices.	
Considered strategies for maintaining support from both school administration and families (for example, schedule activities where parents and students can practice together during family night or send video of yourself demonstrating a practice such as mindfulness or yoga).	

Chapter 4

Assessing Students' Stress Levels and Helping Students Reframe Stress

While being able to implement a variety of stress-reducing strategies is incredibly useful to educators, another essential skill is honing the ability to detect, identify, and assess stress and anxiety levels in students. To gauge overall classroom stress as well as individual student stress, classroom teachers, for example, must be familiar with signs of stress—the specific behaviors that might indicate a child or teen is operating under survival mode. This chapter will outline different "stress signs" to look out for as well as provide some basic assessment tools. The ideas shared are to help educators grow more knowledgeable in their stress-detecting abilities and help evaluate how the implementation of strategies in this book might (or might not) be working. Of course, teachers should not feel pressure to act as counselors or school psychologists and should consult additional help from these trained experts and school administration if needed.

STUDENT STRESS INDICATORS

This section provides a series of behaviors that could indicate a student is experiencing stress or anxiety. Note that "students of any age can show the responses to excessive stress but some responses are more commonly seen at certain ages" (American Psychological Association [APA], 2023, n.p.). These differences will be addressed through explanations of the common stress signs.

Inattention/Restlessness

According to the Child Mind Institute (Ehmke & Schuster, 2023), if a student is squirming in their chair and having trouble paying attention, it could indicate that they are stressed or anxious. While educators and other adults often associate this behavior with attentional challenges (e.g., attention deficit disorder), it may mean that the child or teen has been triggered, and thus, is having a hard time focusing on the teaching and grasping content. Speaking with the parent or family of the student might provide additional information.

Disruptive Behavior

Educators refer to it as "acting out," when a student disrupts class instruction or engages negatively with classmates or the teacher. The root of this behavior might be stress—excess energy produced in the mind–body system that has nowhere to go. When students experience the stress response, they might grow isolated (freeze) or could show aggressive behavior (fight). Unfortunately, this could manifest as kicking chairs, throwing things in the classroom, or even physically attacking other students or adults (Ehmke & Schuster, 2023). Of course, behaviors that can keep students off-task or cause disruptions can manifest differently depending on developmental age (APA, 2023). Children in pre-K and kindergarten might complain of stomachaches or headaches, begin sucking their thumb, or become clingier, while elementary-aged students might cry more often, ask to see the school nurse or become angry, defiant, or laugh excessively. Older students in middle school may also joke more or express anger or opposition, while high school students might shut down, give up on schoolwork, or develop negative coping mechanisms.

Decreased Cognition/Academic Performance

Highly stressed students may stop turning in homework, have trouble paying attention, or be unable to answer questions when called upon. While sometimes confused with a learning disorder, a student experiencing stress or anxiety might suddenly have difficulty with a certain subject or assignment.

Attendance

Not showing up to school could be another indicator of stress or anxiety. Refusing to attend school is pretty common (Ehmke & Schuster, 2023), particularly increasing after vacation or sick days. For students with separation anxiety, leaving home and going to school can be a major issue.

Physical Signs

Stress and anxiety can manifest as physical symptoms and related complaints by students. They might complain of headaches, stomach pains, or rashes. Some students might ask repeatedly to see the school nurse. Of course, we must remember that students, depending on their age, might demonstrate physical manifestations in different ways.

Remember Developmental Differences

For example, middle or high school students may become more withdrawn, socially isolating themselves from groups or cliques they normally associate with or lose motivation to complete classwork or more challenging academic work. They may also become more irritable or fall asleep in class. Younger children may become more whiny or clingy, seeking attention from the teacher or other students.

The following chart (Table 4.1) can be used to help educators keep track of stress-related behaviors in the classroom. For confidentiality reasons, it is recommended that you assign a number or letter for each student and use that instead of a student's actual name. Also, this chart is meant to assist with tracking stress-related behaviors in the context of planning to implement the

Table 4.1. Student Stress Tracker

Student (Recommend using number or letter instead of actual name)	**Stress-Related Behavior** (e.g., loss of concentration/motivation, aggressive behavior, isolation, physical symptoms)	**Possible Intervention**	**Outcome**
Example: Student "A"	Regularly puts head down during morning instruction. Has difficulty answering questions when called on.	Speak with student. Possible phone call to parent. *Invite students to engage in five-minute yoga routine when first entering classroom each day.*	

mind–body methods in this book. It in no way replaces psychological screenings or behavior assessments conducted by school counselors, psychologists, and administrators. If you have concerns about serious behaviors in the classroom regarding a student, you should talk with school administration.

HELPING STUDENTS REFRAME THE WAY THEY THINK ABOUT STRESS

Before diving into the stress-busting, mind–body practices that compose this book, some time should be taken to consider what students might think of stress and to assist them in not only reducing the bad stress but cultivating a healthy relationship with stress. What's meant by relationship is the way they currently view stress, their conditioning and beliefs. While too much negative stress, constantly being triggered, can have damaging effects, students can also learn to be empowered when they experience some degree of stress. K. McGonigal (2015) calls this the "New Science of Stress" (p. xvii). Originally, like many other researchers, McGonigal viewed stress as suffering and something to be entirely avoided. However, one study caused her to question her life's work. The study (Keller et al., 2012) was conducted in 1998 with about thirty thousand Americans, who were asked, "Do you believe stress is harmful to your health?" Eight years later, researchers followed up to find that those with high stress levels experienced a 43 percent increase of premature death—except for those who viewed stress as *not harmful*. They actually had the lowest risk of death, even lower than those who reported experiencing little stress. How we think about stress might be as important or more important than experiencing the stress itself.

Along with sharing stress-management strategies, educators can further these efforts by having conversations with students about stress and how it impacts their lives. Ask them how they perceive stress. To guide them, give them starter stems, such as "When I think of stress, I think of . . . " or "Stress is like . . . " Once you know how students think of stress, you can explain how stress—excessive amounts—might lead to physical and mental challenges, including impacting their schoolwork. But you can provide insight into how stress is an inevitable part of life, and learning to relate to it positively can serve us all well. Here are three beliefs that can aid students in transforming stress (McGonigal, 2015).

Stress Gives Us the Energy to Perform

Stress and anxiety can actually energize us for the task at hand. Students might be able to relate to athletes getting "amped up" before a game, charged with the energy needed to perform at their best and remain competitive. Stress as "energy" can also be discussed in the context of taking exams, the anxiousness can be viewed as energy to provide focus and alertness. Reframing this energy as a resource means viewing "anxiety as excitement, energy, or motivation [which] can help you perform to your full potential" (McGonigal, 2015, p. 104).

Stress Can Make Us More Resilient

While stress can make us angry and more aggressive, stress can also make us more caring, according to the *tend-and-befriend* response (McGonigal, 2015). When stressed, if we focus on helping others, who also might be stressed and suffering, we can better cope with our own stressors. Research suggests that caring for others can increase resilience, changing our biochemistry, and produce feelings of hope and courage. In a study by neuroscientists (Inagaki & Eisenberger, 2012), participants received moderately painful electric shocks while loved ones either held their hand or squeezed a rubber ball. Interestingly, when participants reached out to hold their loved one's hand, activity in their amygdala (recall that this is the brain's alarm system that activates the stress response) decreased while squeezing the ball had no impact on this area. For students, this could mean considering ways to provide care and support for loved ones, friends, and classmates, and during times of stress, rather than withdrawing or acting out, intentionally caring for others as a coping strategy.

Adversity (Past Stress) Can Make Us Stronger

The third reframing you might share with students also comes from McGonigal's (2015) work on developing a positive relationship with stress. Studies also suggest that past stressful experiences make us more resilient to future stress and cultivate a growth mind-set (Seery et al., 2010). When discussing stress and adversity with students, you might ask them to think of a difficult experience—or maybe just a recent problem or disappointment they faced (of course, be skillful here, many students have undergone trauma and we need to be sensitive to bringing up something that might be too intense). Ask them: *What did you do to get through this situation? What strength did you draw upon? What did this experience teach you about how to deal with adversity?*

Chapter 5

Mindful-izing the Classroom

WHAT IS MINDFULNESS AND WHERE DID IT COME FROM?

Mindfulness has become a popular buzzword in recent years. While various definitions exist, "mindfulness" can be considered a psychological trait or quality of awareness (Neale, 2017), or as mindfulness teacher Jon Kabat-Zinn's (2003) popular definition states, "the awareness that emerges through paying attention on purpose, in the present moment, and non-judgmentally to the unfolding of experience moment by moment" (p. 145). Practicing present-moment awareness can help students become more focused, intentional, and less reactive by developing what might be called their "response muscle" (Hall, 2013, p. 14) or a state of mind where they can observe and move beyond conditioned responses that might not be serving them.

While mindfulness is a relatively new phenomenon in the West, it is an ancient practice originating from the Buddhist tradition in India in about 500 BC. The word "mindfulness" is a translation of the Sanskrit word *sati*, and the Pali word *smrit*, which means "to remember" (Gethin, 2011; Neale, 2017, p. 17). While mindfulness has evolved into a separate practice, it is only one of three aspects of training in Buddhism, the other two being the practice of wisdom and ethical behavior. The benefits of mindfulness might be attributed to two distinct but interconnected components (Holzel et al., 2011). First, mindfulness practice helps individuals regulate attention focused on the immediate experience, and second, it encourages our ability to approach the experience with a sense of openness, curiosity, and acceptance.

How Does Mindfulness Reduce Stress and Calm Our Amygdala?

In simplest terms, mindfulness practice over time calms or reduces the amygdala, which we learned is responsible for perceiving "threats" and activating the body's flight-fight-or-freeze response. By becoming more aware of our thoughts and emotions and developing a new relationship with them, we learn to be more skillful in our responses to life's situations and events.

Another approach to understanding how mindfulness reduces stress and anxiety levels is to consider what happens to brain waves when practicing, for example, mindfulness meditation. When a meditator brings awareness to the breath, observing how it flows in and out, but then becomes distracted by thoughts but continues gently coming back to the breath as an anchor, the ordinary "thinking mind" or endless chain of thought is disrupted. Typically, we operate in what is known as beta thinking, a hyper-focused state of alertness. During beta, our brain waves measure 15 to 40 cycles per second. However, when a person practices a meditation technique, their brain shifts to alpha waves (9 to 14 cycles per second). This represents a more relaxed but alert state, like walking through a garden or lying on a beach, listening to ocean waves. In deeper meditation, an individual can enter theta, where the brain waves slow to 5 to 8 cycles per second. As a meditator moves in this direction, neuroscience shows that the brain's arousal levels in the cortex relax, taking "a break from its normal processing of information and conserv[ing] energy" (Jacobs, 2003, p. 129).

How Is Mindfulness Being Implemented in K–12 Schools?

With rising expectations of K–12 students in regard to attention and executive functioning, educators have sought non-traditional ways to help students learn to pay attention and focus. The use of mindfulness in K–12 classrooms has gained significant attention in recent years, due to its potential benefits for students' academic performance, social-emotional regulation, and well-being. According to a Garrison Institute report (2005), schools have been advised to implement mindfulness-based approaches since they are not difficult to learn and may help students become calmer, more responsive, focused, and less stressed—thus creating a positive learning environment. Though mindfulness programs and related curricula have definitely gained popularity, it is difficult to say exactly how many schools or students are utilizing mindfulness, as there is no official reporting system or source. As of this writing, a cursory Google search of "mindfulness and schools" produced 55 million results, up from 4.3 million in 2017.

Unlike Social-Emotional Learning (SEL) and Positive Intervention Behavior Support (PBIS) programs, which teach skills and behaviors from the "outside in," mindfulness-based approaches "teach students from the inside out to cultivate self-management of attention and increase self-awareness by focusing on intrapsychic experiences such as thoughts, emotional states, the breath, and other bodily sensations" (Semple et al., 2017, p. 2). The main goal of most mindfulness-based K–12 programs is to increase awareness of how thoughts and emotions influence speech and behavior, helping students make more appropriate choices (Semple et al., 2010). While a short-term aim might be to enhance learning and academics, a longer-term outcome for students can be the development of positive qualities that benefit individuals and society, such as peacefulness, kindness, generosity, compassion, and patience (Garrison Institute, 2005). While not an exhaustive list, the following are examples of mindfulness-based programs being used in U.S. K–12 classrooms.

Mindfulness-Based Stress Reduction

Originally developed for adults dealing with chronic pain, Mindfulness-Based Stress Reduction (MBSR) has been adapted for K–12 students and generally involves guided meditation, breathing techniques, and other practices to help students manage stress and increase self-awareness.

Mindful Schools

Another popular program is Mindful Schools, which provides curricula and resources to teach mindfulness to K–12 students. Teachers are trained to integrate mindfulness into the classroom through lessons, activities, and guided meditations.

Calm Classroom

Calm Classroom infuses mindfulness methods into the daily school schedule, using short mindfulness activities, breathing, and relaxation techniques.

Mind Up

Created by the Hawn Foundation (actress Goldie Hawn), Mind Up helps students cultivate focus, emotional regulation, and empathy through a combination of neuroscience, positive psychology, and social-emotional learning.

WHAT DOES THE RESEARCH SUGGEST ABOUT MINDFULNESS IN K–12 CLASSROOMS?

Interest in researching mindfulness has grown significantly in recent years. Empirical evidence shows that mindfulness practice can lower stress levels, boost immunity, improve relationships, increase positive emotions and emotional regulation, and sharpen concentration, attention, and memory (Baer et al., 2006; Creswell et al., 2007; Larrivee, 2012; Smalley & Winston, 2010). One of the most notable studies conducted with adults found that thirty to forty minutes of mindfulness practice a day produced structural changes in areas of the brain associated with learning and memory. Researchers found that after eight weeks of practice, participants experienced thickening in the post cingulate, the area of the brain associated with wandering and self-relevance; the hippocampus, which is responsible for learning, memory, cognition, and emotional regulation; and the temporoparietal junction, which is connected to empathy and compassion (Hölzel et al., 2011; Lazar et al., 2005; Pagnoni & Cekic, 2007; Vestergaard-Poulsen et al., 2009). Mindfulness has also been found connected to decreasing activity in the brain's amygdala, where the fear (fight-flight-or-freeze) response is located (Lagopolous et. al, 2009). Another noteworthy study concluded that engaging in regular mindfulness-based practices worked as well to treat anxiety by taking a generic form of Lexapro, a drug commonly prescribed for depression and anxiety (Hoge et al., 2020).

While relatively thinner, research on mindfulness in K–12 classrooms has also been promising. Studies suggest mindfulness programs can enhance school-related skills, including executive function, working memory, sustained attention, and self-regulation (Albrecht et al., 2012; Bellinger et al., 2015; Schonert-Reichl & Lawlor, 2010; Semple et al., 2017). Researchers have found that children, as young as eight years old, have demonstrated benefits in mental health when following guided mindfulness practices using an app at home (Treves et al., 2023). The following section breaks down research findings on mindfulness in K–12 classrooms in various areas.

Attention and Focus

Mindfulness school-based interventions have been found to improve students' focus and attention, reducing what is known as mind-wandering and resulting in better concentration during academic tasks. For example, a k–12study conducted with twenty-five students, ages nine to twelve, practicing Mindfulness-Based Cognitive Therapy, showed participants had significant reductions in parent-rated attention problems (Semple et. al., 2010). Similarly, second- and third-grade students, found to have weaker executive functioning skills, who engaged in Mindful Awareness Practices (MAPs) showed improvements, including in their ability to shift attention (Lee et al., 2008).

Stress and Anxiety

Mindfulness-based programs have also been shown to help students decrease stress and anxiety. The study (Semple et al., 2009) cited above involving twenty-five students ages nine to twelve reported significant reductions in anxiety among children who noted clinically elevated anxiety at baseline. Another example is a study in which thirty-two adolescents with learning disabilities at a private residential school engaged in five to ten minutes of mindfulness meditation at the start of each class period, for five days per week for five straight weeks, revealing decreases in state and trait anxiety (Beauchemin et al., 2008). State anxiety is considered a transitory or fleeting emotional response related to challenging situations in the present moment while trait anxiety lingers and is considered part of one's personality.

Emotional Regulation

Mindfulness interventions assist students in developing greater emotional awareness and regulation. P. C. Broderick and S. Metz (2009) conclude that 120 high school female seniors using a six-session mindfulness program called "Learning to BREATHE" reported reductions in negative emotions and increased emotional regulation, feelings of calmness, and self-acceptance. A more recent study (Hambour et al., 2018) involving 336 Australian high school students, who learned mindfulness techniques, suggests that mindfulness may help teens with dysregulation and social anxiety.

Mental Health

Mindfulness school-based interventions also seem to positively impact the mental health of young people. For instance, research with 55 adolescents between ages thirteen to nineteen in a residential substance abuse program, who learned elements of the Mindfulness-Based Stress Reduction (MSBR) program reported improvements in sleep and reduced worry and mental distress (Bootzin & Stevens, 2005). Another study with 102 adolescents fourteen to eighteen years old in an outpatient psychiatric clinic, after completing an eight-week MBSR intervention showed significant reductions in self-reported anxiety, depression, obsessive symptoms, and other psychological challenges (Biegal et al., 2009).

Social Skills/Relationships

Mindfulness approaches can also enhance social skills in students. The previously mentioned study (Beauchemin et al., 2008) with adolescents at a private residential center found the mindfulness intervention boosted social skills. Research with 214 gifted female high school students suggested a positive relationship between mindfulness practice and social skills (Alfodhly et al., 2021).

Academic Performance

Mindfulness activities were found to help pre-kindergarten students with working memory and planning, and contributed to improved vocabulary and reading scores (Thierry et al., 2016). Researchers reported that high school students learning a mindfulness technique requiring them to recite a sound (mantra) while bringing awareness to their breathing in the stomach performed significantly higher in subjects such as literature and foreign language (Franco et al., 2011).

Note: while these studies show much promise for K–12 classrooms, it's important to note that researchers cite the need for further studies to better understand the best implementation methods, duration of practice, and how other factors impact mindfulness interventions, such as age and developmental stage.

The following section features practical, grade-level-appropriate mindfulness-based strategies you can implement in the classroom. Experiment with them to find what works best with your students to reduce stress and anxiety. The first list is more developmentally appropriate for pre-K–fifth-grade students, while the second list is more suitable for middle and high school students. Of course, regardless of what grade you teach, experiment with the different strategies and activities to find what works best for your students to reduce stress and anxiety and create a positive learning environment.

Mindfulness-Based Strategies for the Elementary Classroom

Before experimenting with mindfulness in your classroom, check out these top tips on implementing mindfulness with children (see Table 5.1).

Heartbeat Exercise

Ask students to do ten to twenty jumping jacks or move the body in some way for one minute. When they finish, guide them to close their eyes, place

Table 5.1. Implementation Tips for Elementary Classroom Mindfulness-Based Strategies

1. Begin a personal mindfulness practice, so you can teach from firsthand experience and serve as a role model of working and interacting from a place of calm and centeredness.

2. Have a regular "mindfulness" time during the school day. For example, the first five-minutes of the day or after recess. Create a routine and be consistent.

3. Keep sessions short.

4. Bring a sense of play and creativity to each mindfulness activity. Make it into a game.

5. If possible, practice mindfulness outdoors, for example, near the school garden or under a tree.

their hand on their heart, listening to their heartbeat, and feel their breathing (source: biglifejournal.com). A variation could be to have students sit or lay on the floor after exercising and place their hands on their heart.

Listen to the Sound

This simple mindfulness activity invites students to listen to the sound of a meditation bowl, bell, or chime. Ask students to sit comfortably and close their eyes (if they want). Instruct them to simply listen to the sound until it disappears. You can have them make a movement when they think the sound is completely faded, such as raising their hand or opening their eyes.

Breathing Buddies

A popular technique, particularly for primary grades, Breathing Buddies involves having students lie down and place a stuffed animal or tennis ball on their stomachs. Have them close their eyes and breathe deeply, watching the stuffed animal or ball rise and fall with each breath. If the object falls, instruct students to simply put it back on their bellies and start again (source: resilienteducator.com).

Body Scan

During this mindfulness activity, students can either sit or lie down as they bring awareness to different parts of the body. For a condensed version, guide them to bring attention to the bottom of their feet, feeling any sensations or tension, then shift awareness to the stomach area, then bring their minds to the neck and shoulder area, again noticing any tension and "breathing into it." Next, ask them to bring awareness to the palms of their hands, experiencing any tingling or warmth. Finally, instruct them to scan their entire bodies. Try adding soothing instrumental music in the background.

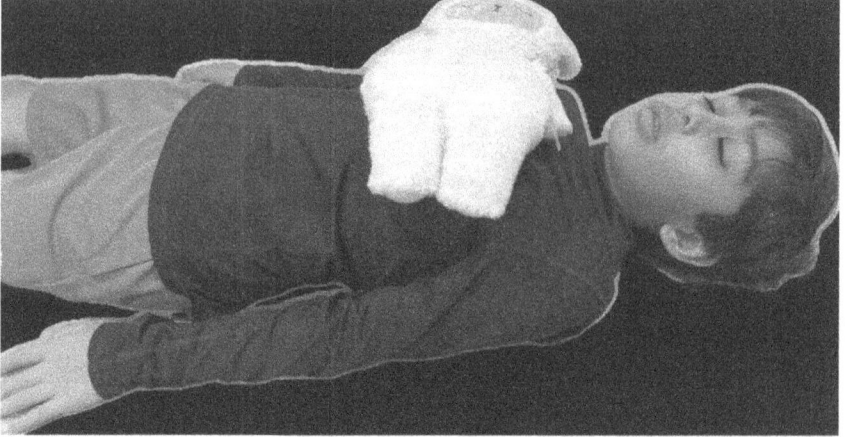

Figure 5.1. Breathing buddies.
Image copyright is owned by author; *Source*: P. N. Patel

Sensory Challenge

Ask students to sit, close their eyes, and take a few deep breaths. Give them the following prompts: For 30 seconds, become aware of any sounds in the classroom, even the faintest noise. During the next 30 seconds, focus on any smells. Then, for the next 30 seconds, tell students to become aware of anything they feel. Finally, ask students to open their eyes and notice anything they see.

Mindful Spoon Challenge

These mindfulness activities require a plastic spoon for each student and a small bowl or cup of water. Have students form a circle, about an arm's length apart. Inform students that their goal is to mindfully pass a spoonful of water around the entire circle without spilling any of it. Have a student take a spoonful of water and transfer the water from their spoon to the student next to them (you can go clockwise). That student then passes the water to the next student and so on, until the water returns to the original student, who then pours it back into the cup or bowl. A simpler variation, which requires less space, is to have students pair up and pass the water back and forth in their spoons.

Mindful Eating

For this activity, you will need a piece of candy such as Skittles or Hershey's Kisses or a raisin or grape for each student. Ask students to use their senses to mindfully explore and eat the item. Begin by having them move the object in their fingers, feeling the texture and shape. Instruct them to also look closely at the object, as if studying it for the first time. Next, have students bring the food to their noses, breathing in any scent. Finish by having students place the food in their mouth carefully without chewing it, for example, allowing the Hershey's Kiss to melt. After a few seconds, they can slowly chew it. Encourage them to sit with the experience after eating the food, noticing any thoughts, emotions, or feelings in their body (source: author).

Drawing the Breath

Pass out a piece of paper to each student and a crayon or colored pencil. Guide students in taking a few deep breaths. Ask them to "draw their breath" by making a line as they breathe in and make another line or mark as they breathe out. Assure them that it doesn't matter how long the line is or whether it is straight or curved. After a few minutes, have them study the lines to see if they notice anything about how they represented their breathing; for instance, did the lines get longer as their breathing deepened?

Calming Glitter Jar

With this mindfulness activity, students focus on a glitter jar or snow globe, allowing their minds to settle as the glitter falls to the bottom. Explain to students that it is natural to have lots of thoughts and sometimes strong emotions, but like the glitter in the jar, they can learn to calm the mind and allow their thoughts to settle down. Shake the jar or globe, set it on a table in the front of the classroom, and invite students to watch the glitter as it settles down. Invite them to imagine their thoughts or feelings calming down as the glitter settles. Students can also make their own mindfulness glitter jars (https://blissfulkids.com/mindfulness-kids-teens-calming-glitter-jar-aka-mind-jar/).

Breathing Boards

Provide each student with a breathing board. Print them out or have students create one. Invite students to practice being mindful of breathing in and out as they trace their finger along the breathing board. Students can use the same board (for example, tracing it a few times) and then move to the next board.

Mindfulness-Based Strategies for the Secondary Classroom

Breath Meditation

During this practice, have middle or high school students sit for one to three minutes and observe their breathing. Begin by inviting students to sit comfortably and close their eyes, if they choose. Guide them to gently bring their awareness to how the breath naturally enters the nostrils and leaves the nasal area. Explain that it is natural to have thoughts or become distracted, and when this happens, to simply return their awareness to the breath. You can use a Tibetan singing bowl, bell, or chime to indicate the beginning and end of the exercise. Also, prior to each mini-meditation, you can have students mentally note their stress or tension levels, from 1 to 5, and then do a quick follow-up assessment after meditating.

Body Scan

The body scan, as explained above in the elementary classroom strategies, is also appropriate for secondary students. Explain to them that getting in tune with the body is a way to become more familiar with how our physical bodies react to the environment and where they hold stress and tension.

Grounding in the Senses

Teach students to mentally ground themselves and become more mindful using the five senses. Known as the 5-4-3-2-1 method, have students take

Figure 5.2. Mindfulness meditation.
Image copyright is owned by author; *Source*: P. N. Patel

a few deep breaths and notice five things around them they can "see." Ask them to "listen" for four sounds in the classroom or environment, "touch" three items around them (e.g., their clothing, a pen, the desk), "smell" two things around them, and "taste" one thing that remains on their tongue (e.g., breakfast, a snack from earlier).

Mindful Listening (with Music)

Take advantage of the fact that middle and high school students become very interested in different genres of music. Select a piece of music, perhaps instrumental, and instruct students to sit with their eyes closed and just listen to the sounds for a minute or two. You can also play the sounds of a nature-based track, such as a thunderstorm or waves crashing on a beach. Ask them to consider what happens to their breathing and bodies as they listen.

Guided Meditation Using Apps

Secondary students might be more inclined to use technology to practice mindfulness. There are a variety of apps that provide guided meditations (some free of charge, others require a subscription). Insight Timer offers a variety of guided meditations you can play for students. Aura is another app that has free resources.

Mindful Doodling

Provide each student with a blank paper and pencil. Ask them to draw three, large circles on the paper. Tell them that when you ring the meditation bell or begin playing music, they will start to draw patterns in the circles. They can make any doodle or design they wish. Guide them in being aware of how they feel during the process, how the pencil feels in their hand, or the sound that the pencil makes as it moves across the paper. If they become distracted, tell them to just come back to making patterns. After a few minutes, ring the bell again or stop the music, indicating that the activity is complete.

Mindful Painting

On the same theme as mindful doodling, you can use paint and straws to engage secondary students in an activity to explore mindfulness and their emotions. Provide students with blank cardstock, watercolor paints, brushes, and straws. Students use the brush to drop paint onto the paper and then blow through the straw to move it around. Cue students to utilize various colors to represent different emotions (e.g., red is anger, yellow is happiness or joy) and notice the sensations in their bodies as they move the paint (source: confidentcounselors.com)

Mindful Spoon Activity

This exercise can also be used with secondary students, with perhaps an adjustment or two. Students can mindfully pass the spoonful of water in a circle. You can also have middle and high school students cultivate mindful listening skills by having them pair up. One student closes their eyes and the partner, using only vocal instructions, must direct them to carefully transfer the water from one spoon to another without spilling any. When finished, students can switch roles.

Chapter 6

Just Breathe! Breathwork Strategies for K–12 Students

WHAT IS BREATHWORK AND WHERE DID IT COME FROM?

"Breathwork" is a term used to describe "intentional and conscious breathing" (Patterson, 2020, p. 16). While we can survive days or weeks without food or water, we can only exist a few minutes without breath. Breathing is fundamental and vital to life and impacts us mentally, emotionally, physically, and spiritually. Breathwork has ancient origins, dating back thousands of years to India, China, and American Indigenous cultures. Conscious use of breath can be found among spiritual traditions around the world, including Sufism, Taoism, Yoga, African healing, and Roman and Druidic traditions (Patterson, 2020). As you will discover in the next chapter, the breath plays an integral role in yoga, tai chi, and qigong, where breathing is synchronized with movement. The breath is also deeply connected with certain mindfulness and meditation practices, such as Buddhist vipassana. While breathwork is often combined with other practices in this book, for example, with many school-based mindfulness and yoga interventions, a separate chapter has been dedicated to its principles and methods so readers gain a deeper understanding and better grasp its nuances for the classroom.

During the twentieth century, more modern approaches to breathwork emerged through the work of Stanislav Grof, who in the 1970s developed the Holotropic Breathwork method. Grof, an LSD researcher, created the technique to access altered states of consciousness using rhythmic patterns of deep breathing. Another breathwork pioneer, Leonard Orr, developed what has become known as Rebirthing Breathwork, which uses conscious connected circular breathing. Since the 1980s, Jessica Dibbs, founder of the

Inspirational Consciousness School, and others, have continued to advance breathwork practice. In recent years, breathwork has gained popularity as an experiential approach to psychotherapy. Breath techniques appear to have wide-ranging, diverse applications, being used in athletic coaching, dentistry, speech therapy, nursing, occupational therapy, military training, and other fields and settings (Brule, 2017).

While researchers note further studies are needed to fully understand its benefits, engaging in breathwork has been shown to reduce stress, anxiety, substance abuse, and depression and help with emotional regulation (Brown & Gerbarg, 2005; Janakiramaiah et al., 2000). Furthermore, studies suggest that breathwork might provide physical benefits, such as decreased physical pain, lower blood pressure, better cardiovascular health, and aid with sleep and digestion. Cognitive benefits include improved focus, concentration, working memory, and cognitive flexibility (Benz & Weiss, 1989; Christiansen, 1972; Fahri, 1996; Rosenberg, Rand, & Asay, 1985; Shaw-Metz, 2023).

In a study by X. Ma and colleagues (2017), adult participants who practiced diaphragmatic breathing, or breathing deeply into the lungs rather than just using the abdomen or rib cage, displayed not only improved respiratory rates but also decreased cortisol levels, the body's main stress hormone. Another study investigating diaphragmatic breathing in adults found a statistically significant decrease in the participant's perceived stress (Sundram et al., 2014). Researchers also found a significant decrease in perceived stress in healthy males, eighteen to thirty years old, who learned alternative nostril breathing (explained further below in the secondary strategies section) (Naik et al., 2018).

How Does Breathwork Reduce Stress and Anxiety (and Calm Our Amygdala?)

Science has established a close connection between the mind and body. For example, breathing is directly connected to our emotional states. Unless specifically trained, a person's breathing patterns under stress are automatic. Negative emotions, such as disgust, trigger breath holding while positive feelings, like laughter, decrease how long we hold our breath (Gilbert, 2002). Thus, breathing patterns correlate with attitudes and how we cope with the environment, and engaging in breathwork can help us with emotional regulation and stress management.

Our fight-flight-or-freeze response activates the sympathetic nervous system, which delivers oxygen to our arm and leg muscles so we can run or fight, but less oxygen goes to our brain's prefrontal cortex, making thinking more difficult. "When you are feeling frightened, in pain, or tense and uncomfortable, your breathing speeds up and becomes shallower" (Andre, 2019). On the other hand, deep breathing activates the parasympathetic nervous system, which tells the brain that we are safe and avoids triggering the stress response (University of Toledo, 2023). In other words, conscious, deep breathing intentionally induces the body's rest and recovery or relaxation response. Research conducted by A. Doll and colleagues (2016) found that intentional, slowed breathing activates the dorsomedial prefrontal cortex and also reduces activity in the amygdala.

How Is Breathwork Being Implemented in K–12 Schools?

Like mindfulness and yoga, breathwork has gained more interest and recognition in schools. Low-cost and generally easy to learn, breathing techniques are now being utilized in conjunction with mindfulness-based interventions, social-emotional learning (SEL) programs, and lessons as brain breaks and energizing activities to keep students alert and focused, and with special populations of students such as those on the autism spectrum. Gauging how many schools or classrooms implement breathwork programs and activities is even more challenging, as this area is often blended with mindfulness-based interventions and other initiatives. While the empirical research around breathwork with K–12 students is limited, a smaller number of studies suggest promising results. Part of the difficulty in disseminating the research findings on breathwork in K–12 schools is that, as explained, breathing techniques are often combined with meditation and yoga interventions, making it difficultto gauge the specific impact of breathing.

Managing Negative Emotions

In a qualitative study with nineteen high school students in a science class, researchers (King et al., 2018) report that deep breathing exercises, which involved the students alternating between guided and unguided breathing for three minutes, placing their hands on their bellies to observe the rising and falling with the breath, promoted emotional regulation and decreasing of negative emotions. D. King and colleagues concluded their research paper by encouraging teachers to "use deep breathing exercises as one possible practice" (p. 212).

Test Anxiety

Breathing techniques have been used as an intervention for test anxiety. H. A. Larson and colleagues (2011) found that high school juniors preparing to take the ACT college admissions test, after practicing deep breathing techniques, showed significant reductions in text anxiety compared to a control group. Another study (Larson et al., 2010) also demonstrated positive results when third-grade students learned elevator breathing (deep, diaphragmatic breathing) to combat text anxiety.

Special Populations

A small number of studies have examined the impact of breathing methods on special populations of students. In a study with four elementary students with attentional difficulties, researchers reported no significant change in reading fluency after the students learned mindful breathing techniques, though one demonstrated better focus and less perceived stress (Idler et al., 2017). A study involving forty-five middle school females of color participating in a six-week after-school program that involved yoga, meditation, and breathing, showed decreased anxiety and better mindful awareness and self-regulation (Berger, 2021).

Breathwork-Based Strategies for the Elementary Classroom

The following breath techniques are more suited for younger students; however, educators may find methods in the secondary section suitable or can modify them for elementary classrooms.

Bumble Bee Breathing

As with mindfulness and yoga-based methods, using animals with breathwork techniques can be a way to engage children. Bee breath takes its name from the buzzing sound made and then exhaling during this method. This technique can be used to help students de-stress and reduce anxiety and negative emotions. Have students begin by covering their ears with their thumbs or hands. Instruct them to inhale through the nose with a soft sound then deeply exhale aloud with a humming sound, like a bee. Have them do this for four to six cycles then sit quietly (source: ekhartyoga.com) (see Figure 6.1).

Buddy Belly Breathing

This technique—also featured in Chapter 4—teaches younger students how to practice belly breathing to calm down and self-regulate using a stuffed toy or prop. To begin, ask students to lie down and place a small stuffed animal, tennis ball, or rolled-up small blanket on their stomach. Gently holding the object, have students fill their bellies with air as you count to three, noticing how the breathing buddy rises up. Direct them to slowly exhale as you count

Figure 6.1. Bumble bee breathing.

to four, watching the buddy fall or slowly sink. Try having students complete five to ten rounds, then ask them how they feel (source: blissfulkids.com).

Bubble Blowing

A fun way to have students practice deeper breathing is to have them be mindful when blowing bubbles. You can find bubble blowers with wands at a lower cost by ordering online or going to local dollar stores. Instruct students to inhale then try to blow a big bubble as they deeply exhale. A variation of this activity is to provide each student with a feather (found easily in arts and crafts stores). Have them breathe in for a count of three, then breathe out trying to move the feather (source: copingskillsforkids.com).

Hot-Air Balloon Breaths

Tapping into elementary students' imagination, have them cup their hands over their mouth, take a deep breath in their nose, then as they blow out through their mouth, expand their hands as if they are inflating a balloon. Have them try a few cycles then sit quietly (source: cosmickids.com).

Washing Machine Breath

Ask students to point their index fingers at one another, slightly over their mouths. After inhaling for three seconds, instruct them to "spin" their index fingers around each other as they deeply exhale (source: cosmickids.com) (see Figure 6.2).

Lotus Breath

Invite students to stand and place their hands together, fingertips touching. Have them keep the pinky fingers and thumbs touching while spreading the three middle fingers out on each hand. Explain that this hand gesture represents the lotus, a beautiful flower that grows in muddy water. Like the lotus, we must often experience challenges and negativity to grow and blossom. From there, instruct students to inhale deeply while raising the lotus flower hands toward the sky. They will then release the hands bringing them down by their sides as they exhale. Repeat for several cycles (source: abcbreathe. org) (see Figure 6.3).

Figure 6.2. Washing machine breath.
Image copyright is owned by author; *Source*: P. N. Patel

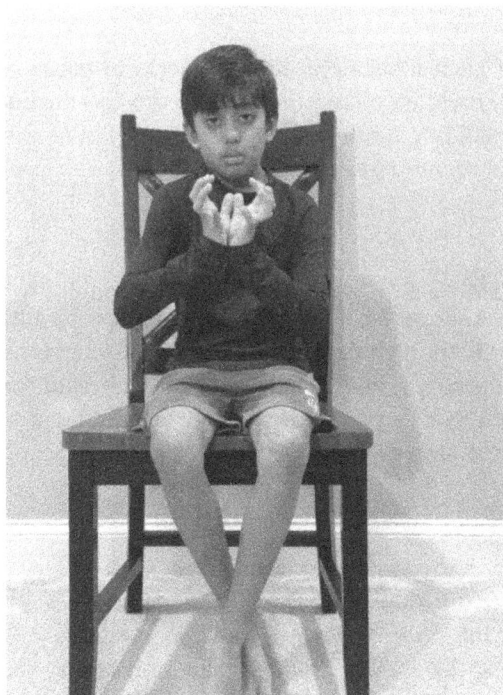

Figure 6.3. Lotus breath.
Image copyright is owned by author; *Source*: P. N. Patel

Breathwork-Based Strategies for the Secondary Classroom

The following are some breathwork techniques to introduce to middle and high school students. It should be noted that there is an overlap between breathing methods for younger students and older ones. Some techniques may work just as well for elementary and secondary. Use your discretion as far as what is age and developmentally appropriate.

Abdominal Breathing

This is an adaptation of the Buddy Breathing method suggested for elementary students. Invite students to sit comfortably (they can also lie down on the floor if space and the condition of the classroom allow). Begin inflating the stomach by inhaling deeply then filling the chest. Students will then exhale, emptying the belly and chest. To help, instruct students to try placing one hand on the stomach to feel how it expands and contracts with the breath. Have students complete several rounds (source: edcuration.com).

Rhythmic Breathing

Near the end of each inhalation, direct students to pause briefly, mentally counting (1, 2, 3) while holding the breath prior to exhaling. Students can experiment with holding for three seconds at the end of an exhalation instead. Complete several rounds (source: edcuration.com).

4-7-8 Exercise

This method can be used when helping students to calm the nervous system. Attributed to Dr. Andrew Weil, the 4-7-8 breath works by sitting comfortably and inhaling slowly through the nose for a count of four seconds, holding the breath for seven seconds, and exhaling out of the mouth for eight seconds. It's recommended that you do no more than four cycles when first learning the method (source: dr.weil.com).

Bellows Breath

To raise energy levels and alertness, have students try this technique. Bellows Breath or the Simulating Breath method involves taking short, rapid breaths through the nose. Have students aim for three in-and-out breaths per second. Do not have them do more than 15 seconds when first learning (source: dr.weil.com).

Box Breathing

A yogic technique used by U.S. Navy SEALs, Box Breathing can help students calm the mind, focus, and activate the parasympathetic nervous system. It is called "Box" Breathing because you breathe and hold for equal counts, following the four equal sides of a box. Ask students to breathe into their nose for a count of four, hold for four seconds, breathe out of their mouth for a count of four, and hold for four seconds. That equals one cycle. Encourage them to try three to four cycles and see how they feel (source: health.clevelandclinic.org).

Alternative Nostril Breathing

Another yogic breathing technique found to promote mental clarity, reduce stress, and activate the parasympathetic nervous system is Alternative Nostril Breathing. The technique requires isolating one nostril at a time and breathing in through one then exhaling through the other. To begin, invite students to sit comfortably, and bring their right hand to their nose, with the index finger hovering over the left nostril while covering the right one with their thumb. Instruct them to inhale through the left nostril while keeping the right one blocked. Then, they will use their index finger to block the left nostril (at this point, both nostrils are closed). The breath is held for a second or two. They will then release the thumb, unblocking the right nostril, and exhale. Keeping the left nostril closed with the index finger, have them inhale through the right nostril. The thumb blocks the right nostril, and again, the breath is held for a count or two. Students will then release their index finger, unblocking the left nostril and exhaling. Have them go through a few cycles of breathing in the left nostril, exhaling out the right, then breathing in through the right nostril and out the left (source: healthclevlandclinic.org) (see Figure 6.4).

Figure 6.4. Alternative nostril breathing.

Chapter 7

Let's Get Moving! Movement-Based Strategies for Students

WHAT ARE MOVEMENT-BASED PRACTICES AND WHERE DID THEY COME FROM?

As with mindfulness, movement-based practices, such as yoga and tai chi, have gained popularity in K–12 classrooms as ways to increase calm and focus, reduce stress and anxiety, and improve health, flexibility, and balance. Movement-based practices generally involve performing slow, controlled movements combined with breathing to increase awareness. An overview of yoga, tai chi, and qigong will be provided before exploring how these practices have been implemented in schools.

Yoga

The practice of yoga is more than five thousand years old, pre-dating Indian traditions, such as Hinduism, Buddhism, and Jainism. The word "yoga" is derived from the Sanskrit word *yuj*, which means to join or unite (as in mind, body, and spirit). With deep roots in Indian philosophy and spirituality, yoga encompasses body postures, breathing, meditation, and ethics. While there are many types of yoga, the main forms are Hatha, the practice of physical movements and postures (the form most associated with yoga), and Raja yoga, which infuses exercise and breathwork with meditation and study (Collins, 2015).

Yoga was introduced to the West in the late nineteenth and early twentieth centuries, as Indian yoga masters traveled to Europe and the United States.

Yoga teachers, such as Paramahansa Yogananda, B. K. S. Iyengar, and Swami Sivananda helped to popularize yoga in the West. In the United States, yoga became mainly a physical fitness practice to increase flexibility, strength, and overall well-being. Scientific studies show that yoga can reduce stress, alleviate anxiety and depression, lower heart rate and blood pressure, and improve physical fitness (National Center for Complementary and Integrative Health, 2013).

How Does Yoga Reduce Stress and Anxiety?

Yoga can reduce stress by activating the parasympathetic nervous system (rest and recover) and help regulate the nervous system in its response to stressors. Through deep breathing, stretching, and relaxation, yoga activates the rest and recovery state (RR), a physiological state of decreased oxygen consumption and reduced blood pressure and heart and respiration rates—the opposite of the body's stress response. Engaging in yoga can increase positive neurotransmitters, such as melatonin and oxytocin, and decrease the stress hormone cortisol (Lim & Cheong, 2015). Like with mindfulness meditation, yoga has been associated with smaller right amygdala volume, the part of the brain responsible for fear and aversion to unpleasant experiences (Gotink et al., 2018). On a deeper level, there is growing evidence that yoga might alter the expression of certain genes and decrease the inflammation that causes stress, aging, and disease (Buric et al., 2017). Research findings suggest that yoga may improve telomeres, the tail end of genes, which fray and shorten over time due to aging, poor nutrition, smoking, chronic stress, and other factors. Practicing yoga can help strengthen and lengthen telomeres (Bevacqua et al., n.d.).

How Is Yoga Being used in K–12 Classrooms?

Like mindfulness practices, yoga has increasingly been implemented in schools in various ways. While there is currently no standard national curriculum, yoga methods have been embedded in physical education classes; school counseling and wellness programs; and after-school programs and clubs as short brain breaks between classes and subjects; as well as integrated into mindfulness programs. To give a sense of its popularity, researchers completing a summary of yoga in K–12 schools, identified thirty-six programs in more than 960 schools across the United States, with more than 5,400 trained instructors (Butzer et al., 2015). There are several popular yoga-based programs used in schools, including Yoga Calm, YogaKids, Kidding Around Yoga, and Yoga Ed.

Advocates insist that yoga practices help educators address school reform goals to educate the whole child and enhance social-emotional development (Hyde & Spence, 2013). Scientific research suggests yoga provides students with many academic, social, and emotional benefits. More specifically, researchers posit that yoga practices can cause changes in brain structure and function, enhancing skills such as self-regulation and prosocial behavior, which results in improved academic performance (Hagins & Rundle, 2016).

Stress Reduction/Enhanced Mental Health

Yoga can serve as a vehicle to help K–12 students de-stress and cope with anxiety and other mental challenges. In their work with forty-nine high-stressed students in an alternative education school in an inner-city district, researchers found that a transformative life skills program, which involves teaching yoga postures (asanas), breathing, and meditation, produced significant reductions in stress, anxiety, and depression (Frank et al., 2014). Yoga can also have a positive impact on students' mental health and well-being. For example, in one study at a rural public high school, ninth-grade students participating in four-to-five yoga sessions over two weeks self-reported decreases in perceived stress (though a reduction in depression could not be confirmed) (Beets & Mitchell, 2010).

Improved Physical Health

As with the general population, students practicing yoga can improve their balance, flexibility, and strength; reduce their body mass index (BMI); and improve cardiovascular fitness. Researchers, Benavides and Caballero (2009), reported that after a twelve-week yoga program, Hispanic children and teens at risk for type 2 diabetes due to weight became more involved in physical activities and lost weight. Another example of yoga's physical health benefits for students comes from Seo and colleagues' (2012) research, where they found that yoga training for twenty Korean boys classified as obese increased their heart rates, muscular strength, and flexibility, causing weight loss and improved body mass index.

Prosocial Behavior

Yoga-based interventions have been shown to promote positive behaviors and interactions among students and reduce negative, unwanted behaviors such as bullying. In a study of 104 third-through-fifth-grade students at five Detroit public schools, researchers reported that, after engaging in weekly yoga sessions during physical education classes, bullying behaviors among students decreased as well as stress levels (Centeio et al., 2017).

Improved Academic Performance

By reducing stress and enhancing cognitive abilities, such as attention and concentration, yoga might also boost academic performance. In their research, A. Kauts and N. Sharma (2009) found that high schools participating in a seven-week, one-hour-a-day yoga module performed better in math, science, and social studies than classmates who did not practice yoga. Yoga has also been a proposed intervention for children with attentional challenges, such as those diagnosed with attention deficit disorder. Studies suggest such interventions help students with attention problems to concentrate and self-regulate (e.g., Harrison, Manocha, & Rubia, 2004; Peck et al., 2005; Redfering & Bowman, 1981).

Students with Special Needs

With a focus on mind–body integration, educators have also experimented with yoga as a vehicle to help students with developmental disabilities, including Down syndrome, attention deficit hyperactivity disorder (ADHD), autism spectrum disorder, and sensory integration issues. For instance, yoga can provide benefits to children with cerebral palsy by strengthening and stretching various muscles and tendons, realigning the spine, and granting a greater range of movement (Mockford & Caulton, 2008).

Tai Chi

Tai chi (pronounced "tie chee") is a four-hundred-year-old Chinese martial art, which has evolved into a holistic health system and form of low-impact, gentle exercise. Translated as "grand ultimate fist," tai chi chuan is a system of combat, a form of Chinese boxing, created during the Ming Dynasty by General Chen Wangting, who combined principles of Chinese medicine, breathing, and fighting techniques (Figueroa & Berwick, 2012). Today, the words "tai chi" likely conjure up seniors in the park in the early morning hours, waving their hands slowly and adjusting their feet. Tai chi is based on yin and yang, the Taoist theory of polar, dynamic opposites. Thus, tai chi utilizes slow and fast, hard and soft movements while combining the breath to develop *chi* or internal energy.

Qigong

Qigong (pronounced "chee" "gong") might be considered the older sibling of tai chi. An ancient, mind–body health system, qigong's origins are slightly more mysterious, dating back thousands of years. Qigong is believed to have been created by Chinese shamans and healers based on Taoist principles, and unlike tai chi, was designed solely for health, peace, and longevity as opposed to combat. Mentions of the term "qigong" can be found in Taoist literature dating back to the Tang Dynasty (AD 618–907). Qi, meaning "energy or life force," and gong, translating to "work" or "cultivation," qigong means to work with or systematically develop one's inner energy to promote circulation and balance. Like tai chi, there are various styles or variations of qigong. While sharing some commonalities, tai chi differs from qigong in the sense it was specifically developed as a martial art. Also, tai chi features sequenced movements or forms, which require a bit more range of movement, while qigong movements are generally performed in a static position or in a smaller radius.

Substantial research has been done on tai chi and qigong, predominately conducted with adult populations. Both practices provide a host of physical and psychological benefits.

Health Benefits

While not requiring weight training or resistance, tai chi and qigong contributed to positive impact on bone health (Maddalozzo & Snow, 2000), improved cardiovascular health and lower blood pressure (Young et al., 1999), and enhanced physical functioning, including for elderly practitioners (Li et al., 2001). Other studies, such as those with tai chi, suggest practitioners enjoy improved immunity, decreased insomnia, and less inflammation.

Psychological Benefits

Tai chi and qigong also boosted self-efficacy and the perceived ability to deal with stress and new experiences (Kutner et al., 1997). Furthermore, regular practice could decrease stress, anxiety, and depression (Fransen et al., 2007).

How Do Tai Chi and Qigong Reduce Stress and Anxiety?

Think of tai chi and qigong as mindfulness in motion or "meditation on wheels" (Wayne interviewed in Heid, 2017, n.p.). The slow, flowing movements gently stretch and twist our bodies, releasing tension in the process. Dr. Michael Irwin, a professor of behavioral sciences and director of the Mindful Awareness Research Center at UCLA, who has extensively studied the benefits of tai chi, explains that it reduces stress partly due to the soothing effects the activity has on the sympathetic nervous system (SNS), which is triggered under stress. Similarly to aerobic exercise, like brisk walking or jogging, tai chi increases hormone and heart rate measures associated with lower SNS activity (Heid, 2017).

How Are Tai Chi and Qigong Being Used in K–12 Schools?

Rather than take up Tai Chi, children generally gravitate toward more active martial arts, such as Karate or Tae Kwon Do. Research on how tai chi and qigong are being used in schools is limited and less available than mindfulness and yoga. One early study conducted by Baron (1998) with elementary students learning tai chi did not report positive outcomes. In a study conducted at a Boston middle school, students met one hour per week to learn tai chi movements and Mindfulness-Based Stress Reduction (MSBR) activities and self-reported experiencing calmness, improved sleep, and less reactivity (Wall, 2005). A twelve-week study of introducing elementary students to tai chi found that it improved pulmonary function and reduced breathing problems, including for those with asthma (Lin et al., 2017). In a smaller study, adolescents diagnosed with ADHD displayed less hyperactivity and anxiety and improved conduct after participating in a five-week tai chi intervention, according to teachers (Hernandez-Reif et al., 2001).

The following section outlines activities and ideas for implementing yoga, tai chi, and qigong in the elementary and secondary classrooms.

MOVEMENT-BASED STRATEGIES FOR THE ELEMENTARY CLASSROOM

Before reviewing and implementing the various movement-based strategies with elementary students, check out Table 7.1, which provides tips on implementation and ensuring your approach is developmentally appropriate.

Classroom-Friendly Yoga Poses (for Elementary Students)

There are a number of simple yoga poses recommended for the elementary classroom that do not require large amounts of space or time. Here are some poses to get started with students:

Mountain Pose

Have students stand straight up, arms to the side, with palms facing outward. Tell students to stand tall, like a tree, or imagine they are strong, like

Table 7.1. Implementation Tips for Elementary Classroom Movement-Based Strategies

1. Set norms and expectations prior to beginning the activities. Have clear, reasonable consequences (e.g., if you are making contact with a classmate or moving out of your space, you will sit out for the pose).

2. It's okay to be less precise with instructions; keep the flow and engagement going. Students will generally pick up the movements over time.

3. Appeal to the imagination, creativity, and sense of play of children. Use stories, music, games, images, animals, props, and characters.

4. Keep movements and sequences shorter to maintain attention.

5. Whenever possible, model the movements, poses, or activities for students. Do the movements *with* the children.

a mountain. Invite them to take a deep breath and raise their arms so their palms are parallel to their ears, then lower their arms and release the breath (source: positive psychology.com).

Warrior Pose

Invite students to move into a lunge position, placing one foot back and one foot forward. Ask them to bend their front knee while placing their palms together over their head with arms straight. If possible, they can look up.

Figure 7.1. Warrior pose.
Image copyright is owned by author; *Source*: P. N. Patel

Chair Pose

Ask students to begin in Mountain Pose. As they inhale, direct them to reach their arms up and connect the palms. As they exhale, students will bend their knees, as if sitting in a chair, and try to get their thighs parallel to the floor. The knees will slightly reach over the toes (source: Collins, 2015).

Cat/Cow Pose

For this pose, students begin on their hands and knees with the back straight. As they breathe in, they bring in their tummy and arch the back up (like a cat stretching). Breathing out, they move to the cow pose by moving the belly down and lifting the chest and head (source: Collins, 2015).

Child's Pose

Instruct students to begin on all fours, in a tabletop position. They will take a deep breath in, and then encourage them as they exhale to push or slide their arms forward, palms facing downward. Their arms will straighten (source: positivepyschology.com).

Gamifying Yoga

An engaging approach to embedding yoga into the elementary classroom is to turn it into a game. One idea is to play Yogi Says (like Simon Says), where the teacher says different commands, such as "go into tree pose" and students must listen for the word "Yogi" first then assume the pose as the teacher does it. Another strategy to gamify yoga is to use music and play a sort of freeze dance. Play some music and when it stops students must assume a certain yoga pose. For primary students, you can have a box of stuffed animals and as you pull out a toy, ask the students to assume a pose they think the animal might make. Finally, educators can use storytelling to engage students in yoga, reading from picture books and inviting students to try various poses featured in the book (source: gogoyogakids.com). There's no shortage of yoga books for young children. Some popular titles include *Smile with Yoga*, *Our Families Doing Yoga*, *Yoga Animals*, *Yoga at the Zoo*, and *Good Morning Yoga*.

Below are some additional ideas to gamify yoga:

- Mirror Mirror: Pair students up. One student slowly performs a yoga pose and a classmate must try to mimic the movements. Switch leaders (source: gogoyogakids.com).

- Body Shapes: Draw a pose on the whiteboard. Students must try to make that shape with their bodies (source: gogoyogakids.com).
- Yoga Pose Cards: You can purchase a variety of yoga flashcards, which have a pose or activity on them. The teacher draws a card then students must complete that pose or task.

Tai Chi Activities for Elementary Students

While tai chi might be popular with seniors, educators can still present it in high-energy, engaging ways. Here is a simple exercise you can try with children.

Single-Arm Silk Reeling

Invite students to stand and place their left hand on their hip as they sink their weight onto their left foot. Next, they raise their right arm (slowly) with the palm facing up. They will step the right foot out wider, and keeping weight on the left leg, "wipe" their right arm to their right side as they transfer weight onto the right leg (source: Figueroa & Berwick, 2012).

Standing with the feet together, have students pivot their right foot out slightly and shift weight to the right leg. Step the left foot out. Ask students to gently bring their arms out to the right side of the body as if "pushing" to the right. Arms should be chest high. With weight on the right leg, students will side-swipe with both arms to their left. As their hands pass the right hip, they will transfer weight to the left leg. So the hands are gliding from the right to the left (source: Figueroa & Berwick, 2012).

Figure 7.2. Single arm silk reeling.
Image copyright is owned by author; *Source*: P. N. Patel

MOVEMENT-BASED STRATEGIES FOR
THE SECONDARY CLASSROOM

To ensure the movement-based strategies you try with middle and high school students are developmentally appropriate and engaging, review Table 7.2.

Classroom-Friendly Yoga Poses (for Teens)

Below are some basic yoga poses you can use with secondary students. Of course, you can experiment with poses featured above under the "Classroom Friendly Yoga Poses (for Elementary Students)" section; however, this section will list additional poses that are slightly more advanced or require continuous sequencing.

Butterfly Pose

Students begin by sitting on the floor and bringing the soles of their feet together, keeping the spine straight. Grab the bottom of each foot and place the elbows against each thigh. Invite students to feel the gentle pull on the hamstrings and hips as they exhale slowly (see Figure 7.3) (source: tummee.com).

Table 7.2. Implementation Tips for Secondary Classroom Movement-Based Strategies

1. Set norms and expectations prior to beginning the activities. Have clear, reasonable consequences. Also, provide a sense of structure. For example, use the same opening and closing sequence or activity. Also remember that secondary students might have heightened self-consciousness. Keep this in mind when establishing the physical layout and format. For example, students might not feel comfortable with classmates behind them. A circle format can feel more inviting and comfortable.

2. Provide middle and high school students with a choice. Perhaps offer a few choices of what poses they practice. Also, consider offering other options for students not comfortable with performing yoga or other movement-based activities, including journaling, sitting meditation, quiet time, or arts-based activities.

3. Older students will want to know *why* they should engage in these types of activities. Share short examples of research, including those done with secondary students. Show visuals of what kind happen to the brain when engaging in yoga, tai chi, or qigong.

4. Create a soothing environment. Consider playing calming, instrumental music in the background. Perhaps dim the lights. Consider setting up yoga matts and cushions.

5. Be encouraging and lighten up with teens. Be playful, laugh, enjoy. Give students space to come around and engage.

Figure 7.3. Butterfly pose.
Image owned by author; *Source*: Joel Neimann

Standing Forward Pose

To perform this pose, have students inhale then exhale and bend forward at the hips (not the waist). Instruct them to bring their hands and fingertips to the floor slightly in front of their feet. If they cannot reach, students can cross their forearms and hold their elbows. Encourage them to inhale and on the exhale gently stretch downward—of course, easily and knowing their limits so as to not cause injury. Have them hold the pose for 30 to 60 seconds, then tell them to inhale and come up slowly to a standing position (source: mom-junction.com).

Tree Pose

With this yoga pose, students shift their weight to one side and then place the bottom of one foot on the inside of the opposite thigh or calf. Invite the students to place their palms together at chest level. Remind students to gently focus on the in and out breath as they hold the pose (source: positive-pyschology.com).

Figure 7.4. Tree pose.
Image owned by author; *Source*: Joel Neimann

Eagle Pose

A slightly more challenging pose, Eagle Pose can help challenge students and increase their balance and focus. From a standing position, ask students to bend their knees and cross their left thigh over their right one, hooking the top of their left foot behind their right calf. They will then tuck their right elbow into the crook of their left arm, touching their palms, with fingers pointing toward the ceiling. See if they can hold this pose and concentrate on their breathing for 30–69 seconds (source: yoga journal.com).

Savasana

This pose is often used to end a yoga session and can help middle and high school students learn to take time to relax, rest, and rejuvenate. Invite them to lie on their backs, with their eyes closed, legs comfortably apart, and palms facing up. Have them bring awareness to their breathing, observe it, and allow each part of their body to deeply relax (without falling asleep). Do this for a minute or two (source: verywellfit.com).

Sun Salutation

This sequence of poses comes from Vinyasa, a popular, flow style of yoga, which combines movements, providing many of the benefits of yoga (e.g., flexibility, balance, focus, relaxation) in a relatively short period of time. This might work better with older students, but of course, can be adapted for elementary students as well. Sun Salutation consists of twelve poses, and the breath is very important during each pose. Movement from one pose to the next is always done in conjunction with either inhalation or exhalation. Also, remind students to know their limits so as to avoid injury, and demonstrate some modifications for students who are unable to physically perform a particular move (source: verywellfit.com). Below is a brief description of how to perform each pose (source: veryfitwell.com).

Mountain Pose

Invite students to stand, with feet about shoulder-length apart. As they inhale, they bring their arms out to the side, above their head, palms together. Lift the gaze to their palms.

Forward Bend

Exhaling, with arms coming to the side, students will bend forward as if doing a swan dive into a pool. Students can touch or reach toward the floor with their fingers. If this is difficult, instruct them to bend their knees slightly.

Plank Pose

After inhaling and straightening up, encourage students to plant their palms on the ground and either step back or jump back, making a plank with their bodies. The goal is to create a straight line from the crown of the head to the heels. Remind students here to inhale.

Knees, Chest, and Chin Pose

Exhaling, students will lower their knees, chest, and chin to the floor. The idea is to keep the behind raised and elbows hugging the ribs.

Cobra Pose

Inhaling, with hands planted on each side, direct students to lift their head toward the sky. The toes should be pointed, with the tops of the feet aligned with the ground.

Downward Facing Dog

As they exhale, students will push their bodies back, with the bottom toward the sky, head down, arms extended. Have them take a few breaths in this pose.

Forward Bend Pose

Tell students to inhale as they raise their heads and step the right foot next to the left, moving upward into a forward bend.

Mountain Pose

Students will inhale, raising up straight, back to mountain pose. Encourage them to exhale and become aware of their breath and body.

Chair Qigong

Another movement-based activity suitable for both elementary and secondary students is a curriculum called Chair Qigong, which was created by the author and then-undergraduate education major Audrey Mecklenburg at Wesleyan College in Macon, Georgia. Looking for a way to make qigong more student-and-classroom-friendly, they worked with an experienced qigong instructor to develop eight simple movements that combine motion and breath and could be done sitting in a chair at a classroom desk. Chair Qigong, used by educators across the country, can be done during morning meetings, during brain breaks, or while transitioning to different subjects or classes to help students de-stress, focus, and re-energize. The sequence takes little time to perform all the right movements; however, students can also complete movements separately if time doesn't allow.

The following section breaks down each Chair Qigong movement. Note: all movements are performed from a seated position; however, they can easily be adjusted if students have more space to stand in the classroom, or Chair Qigong can be completed outside, for instance, during recess.

Reach for the Moon

In this first movement of the sequence, from a seated position, students breathe in and stretch their arms up over their heads, with palms facing up. They then exhale when the arms are fully extended and begin to come back down. You can have students perform several rounds of the movement.

Figure 7.5. Reach for the moon.

Archer's Pose

Students breathe in, bringing their hands up past the chest. As they exhale, they then look to the left, extending the left hand outward as far as possible and drawing the right hand back, as if they were pulling back a bow to shoot an arrow. Ask them to then switch sides, extending the right hand, looking toward their right, and drawing back the left hand.

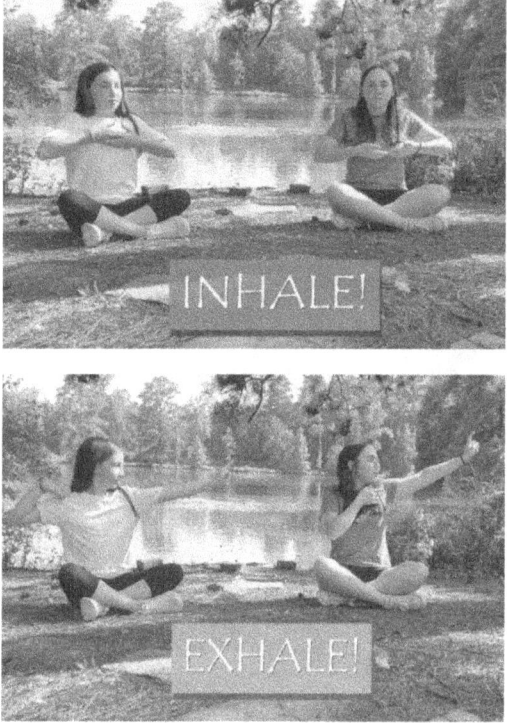

Figure 7.6.   Archer's pose.

Splitting the Atmosphere

During this movement, students will inhale deeply and raise the right hand toward the sky, palm inverted upward, as they slowly push down with the opposite hand (palm facing the ground). Switch hands on the next round.

Figure 7.7.   Splitting the atmosphere.

Wise Owl Turns Head

Breathing in, students gently turn their head to the left while expanding the chest and shoulders and turning their hands so the palms face away from them. As they exhale, they return to center. Switch sides.

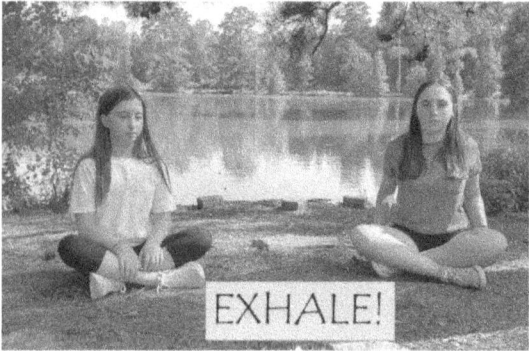

Figure 7.8.   Wise owl turns head.

Around the World

Students inhale and slowly turn their bodies clockwise. Exhaling, they circle their bodies back in the opposite direction. The palms remain on the upper thighs for support and the head is facing downward as they circle to the lowest point.

Figure 7.9. Around the world.

Touch the Earth

During this movement, students start by bending down and reaching their hands toward their feet or ankles. Inhaling, they slowly rise up, tracing their hands along the back of their legs. Exhaling, they bend back down, tracing their hands along their legs toward the back of their ankles. Repeat.

Figure 7.10. Touch the Earth.

Pushing Out the Negative

This movement looks like students are throwing slow-motion karate punches. Breathe in and exhale, slowly extending the right fist. Then, they open their right hand and pull it in as they extend their left fist. Again, the left fist opens, grabs, and draws in as the right fist goes out.

Figure 7.11.   Pushing out the negative.

Rise, Hold, and Release

In the final movement of the sequence, students slowly stand in place (rising on the balls of the feet if they can) while inhaling, then exhaling, drop their body weight down, letting go of any stress or tension.

Figure 7.12.   Rise, hold, and release.

Chapter 8

The Vagus Nerve?

WHAT IS THE VAGUS NERVE AND
HOW DOES IT WORK?

The "vagus" nerve (pronounced like "Vegas" as in Las Vegas), is the tenth cranial nerve in the body. It is the longest and most complex of the twelve cranial nerves, reaching from our brain stem to various organs in the body, including the heart, lungs, digestive system, and respiratory system. Through sensory and motor fibers, the vagus (or vagal) nerve sends information from the organs back to the brain and from the brain to operate each organ. The vagus nerve is the main component of the parasympathetic nervous system and oversees the functioning of internal organs, including digestion, heart rate, breathing, immune response, and cardiovascular activity. Regarding stress and anxiety, the vagus nerve plays a major role. Through this nerve, our bodies continuously report back to our brain, letting it know whether to remain in a stress state or shift to a relaxed, parasympathetic state. Everything from how we emotionally express ourselves, to how we breathe, to what we digest, provides a literal feedback loop for how our bodies should respond. As you can see, the vagal nerve is incredibly important in our quest to understand how to help students self-regulate and experience calm in the classroom.

While research on the vagus nerve has gained significant attention in recent years, examination of the topic goes back as early as the 1930s. Researchers conducted lab experiments with animals to see how vagus nerve stimulation (VNS) impacted different parts of the brain (Bailey & Bremer, 1938; Foley & DuBois, 1937). Research continued through the subsequent decades, and in 1998, VNS was modernized with the first human implant for the treatment of epilepsy (George et al., 2000). Originally, the vagus nerve was considered strictly a parasympathetic "outward" nerve that controls and regulates automatic functions like heart rate; however, it has been redefined as a mixed nerve with 80 percent inward sensory fibers that deliver information to the brain from the head, neck, thorax, and stomach (George et al., 2000). VNS technology has been compared to a pacemaker for the heart. A stimulator is surgically implanted under the skin of the chest, and a wire is connected to the left vagus nerve. Electrical impulses are sent through the vagus nerve to the brain stem. There are also more advanced, non-invasive stimulators being used, for example, one device that is held to the back of the neck (Yu & Wang, 2023).

While researchers note that this area is an evolving field and additional work needs to be done to better understand the topic, studies suggest that VNS might treat anxiety, depression, digestion problems, inflammation and autoimmune disorders, and stress. Furthermore, vagal nerve stimulation could produce cognitive benefits, such as improved mental functioning and working memory. Researchers found that when administering VNS to patients with major depressive disorders, 40 percent (12/30) experienced an improvement in mood after twelve weeks of treatment (Rush et al., 2000). In a later study, S. M. Chavel and colleagues (2003) reported lower anxiety in epilepsy patients who underwent VNS treatment, which was believed to be a secondary benefit of reduced seizures. While further studying patients in the Rush and colleagues study, researchers (Sackeim et al., 2001) noted improvements in their motor speed, psychomotor function, and executive function but could not conclude that VNS had directly enhanced cognitive function since these changes were correlated with improvements in depressive symptoms. Research continues to be conducted on VNS as a potential treatment for bipolar disorder, Alzheimer's, disease, obesity, and other conditions.

How Does the Vagal Nerve Reduce Stress and Calm the Nervous System?

To grasp how working with the vagus nerve can assist in stress and anxiety management, we need to return to the body's fight-flight-or-freeze response. This evolutionary response has helped our ancestors survive during times when life was extremely dangerous, for example, when a wild animal could spring out from behind the bushes at any time. While we are generally not under constant threat in modern times, our sympathetic nervous system can still be triggered by any "perceived threat." Continuous triggering of this stress response can wear out the mind–body system and cause health problems and other conditions. The parasympathetic nervous system's role is to return us to a stable, regulated state. This occurs when the vagus nerve sends a signal to the brain that there is no longer a threat, and that we are not in danger. Breathing and heart rate slow, muscles relax, digestion returns, and we enter a rest and recovery state. The vagus nerve, therefore, is crucial in keeping us from living in a constant, anxious, survival mode.

Basic living strategies such as exercise, eating right, and getting enough sleep activate the vagus nerves (Cleveland Health Clinic, 2023). However, there are additional natural actions we can take to further strengthen the vagus nerve, what is known as "vagal toning" or our resilience to stress and the ability to recover from the stress response. These strategies include meditation, mindfulness, yoga, tai chi (the main practices in this book), biofeedback, and spending time in nature. According to Dr. Yufang Lin, director of education, Wellness, and Preventive Medicine at the Medical Outpatient Center in Ohio (in Cleveland Health Clinic, 2023), vagal tone is often measured by checking one's heart rate variability, or the variation in time between your heartbeats. A stronger vagal tone means your heart rate variability is higher—which indicates balanced responses to the environment through both the sympathetic and parasympathetic nervous systems.

The Impact of Meditation, Yoga, and Tai Chi on the Vagus Nerve

Activities, such as yoga and breathwork appear to directly stimulate the vagus nerve by activating the parasympathetic nervous system. While additional research is needed to better understand the process, a review of studies found that practitioners of meditation, yoga, deep breathing, and relaxation techniques displayed "vagal dominance" during and after sessions (Tyagi & Cohen, 2016). In particular, yoga seemed to increase vagal toning in practitioners compared to non-practitioners, including sedentary individuals and those who engaged in aerobic exercise (Friis & Sollers, 2013; Satin et al., 2014). B. E. Kok and colleagues (2013) also reported that participants who practiced Loving-Kindness Meditation, a Buddhist-inspired technique that involves self-generating positive emotions, experienced increased perception of social connection, which in turn, improved vagal tone.

HOW IS VAGUS NERVE "ACTIVATION" BEING USED IN K–12 SCHOOLS?

As of this writing, there is little or no research investigating the use of VNS or direct vagus nerve "activating" strategies in K–12 schools. Generally, the topic is approached from the angle of assisting students in self-regulating their nervous system and, consequently, the vagus nerve through yoga, mindfulness-based activities, and lessons. Clinical practitioners, such as therapist Deb Dana featured in a two-part YouTube interview, (S'Cool Moves, 2019) have addressed vagus nerve stimulating exercises within the context of guiding K–12 students in understanding their nervous systems and regulating emotions and stress. In her book *The Polyvagal Path to Joyful Learning*, D. E. Wilson (2023) frames the use of vagal-activating exercises using what is known as the Polyvagal Theory, a framework proposed by Stephen Porges in 1994 and later popularized by Dana. In the book, Wilson infuses polyvagal theory principles into working with K–12 students, helping them "befriend their nervous system." While not endorsed by some in the neuroscientific community, who argue the theory is not empirically substantiated (Grossman & Taylor, 2007; Neuhuber & Berthoud, 2022), the Polyvagal Theory posits a third type of nervous system response—in addition, to the sympathetic and parasympathetic nervous systems. In this view, the parasympathetic nervous system can be further divided into two distinct branches: a ventral vagal pathway, which supports social engagement, and a dorsal vagal pathway, which supports immobilization or "shutdown." Through what is called "neuroception," our nervous systems unconsciously constantly look for and respond to cues of safety or danger, causing us to enter various states.

In applying the Polyvagal Theory to classrooms, the idea is to teach students to understand their nervous systems by visualizing three different states that they might experience—moving up and down what is known as the autonomic ladder. When we are at the top of the ladder, in the ventral vagal state, we feel safe, connected, mindful, and regulated. However, when slipping into the sympathetic state, our stress response is triggering, making us want to "fight" or "take flight." When experiencing the bottom rung or dorsal vagal state, we feel overwhelmed and shut down, wanting to withdraw or isolate. To help students understand and remember, colors can be assigned to each of the three states, for example, a soothing green color for ventral vagal, a yellow color for sympathetic (caution or on alert), and a light blue (freeze) for dorsal vagal. Educators can also associate kid-friendly visuals, such as animals, with each nervous system state. In this case, a turtle withdrawing its head could represent the dorsal vagal state, while fish darting away from a shark or predator could symbolize the sympathetic fight-or-flight state, and a bear cub cuddling with its mother perhaps serve as the connected ventral vagal state. Dana (S'cool, 2019) suggests having students use physical objects, such as colored beach stones, to represent what nervous system state they are experiencing at the moment. With a conceptual understanding of their nervous system, students could then be positioned to learn various polyvagal "exercises" to enhance a state of safety and connection.

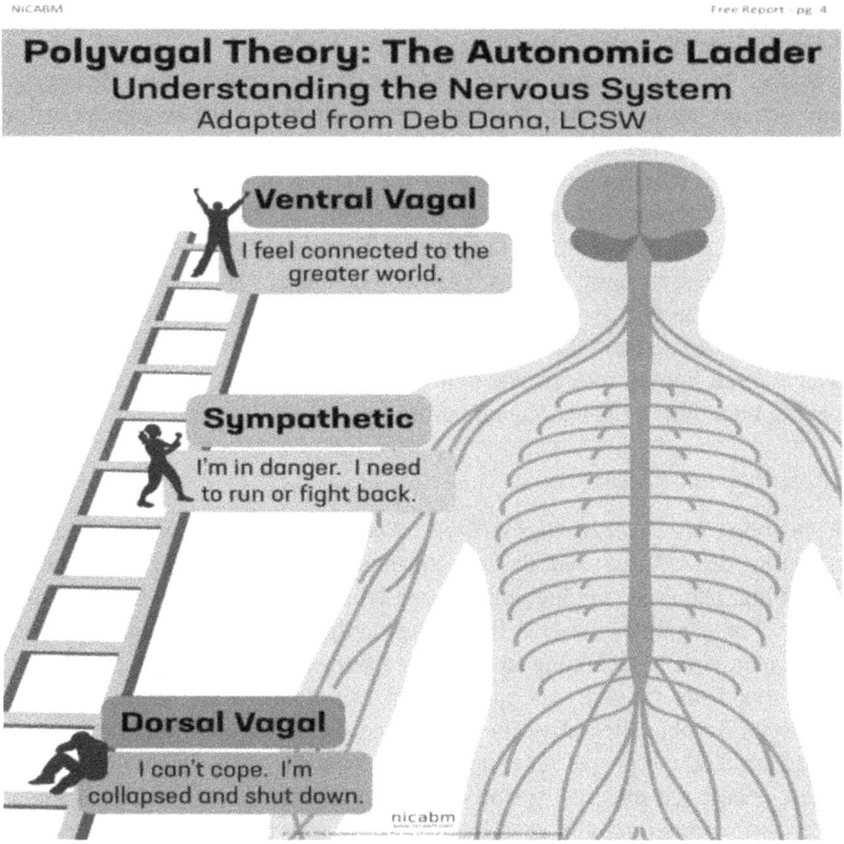

Polyvagal Theory: The Autonomic Ladder
Understanding the Nervous System
Adapted from Deb Dana, LCSW

Ventral Vagal
I feel connected to the greater world.

Sympathetic
I'm in danger. I need to run or fight back.

Dorsal Vagal
I can't cope. I'm collapsed and shut down.

nicabm

Figure 8.1. Polyvagal Autonomic Ladder.
NICABM: https://www.nicabm.com/mapping-nervous-system-response/

Vagal-Toning and Polyvagal-Based Strategies for the Classroom

While research continues on the topic, educators might experiment in small ways with trying various classroom-friendly exercises to activate vagal toning to increase and enhance feelings of calm, safety, and connection in their classrooms. Although many of the strategies presented in this book, such as yoga and breathwork, align with vagal toning, here are some additional polyvagal exercises you can try with K–12 students.

Loving-Kindness Meditation

As noted earlier in this chapter, practicing Loving-Kindness Meditation could boost vagal tone. Inform students that Loving Kindness Meditation involves sending positive feelings or "vibes" of loving-kindness to oneself and others from a meditative state. The following is a condensed version that can be practiced in the classroom. Have students sit comfortably, close their eyes, and become aware of their breathing. Invite them to shift awareness to the heart area. Ask them to think of someone (or something, such as a pet, character, or image) that instantly elicits positive feelings or makes them smile. Tell students to imagine their person or thing sitting in from of them. What feelings would they experience in their heart? Then, on each out-breath, students mentally repeat a phrase such as "may you be happy," or "may you be well," and imagine an energy of loving-kindness is flowing from their heart to the object. Explain to them that they can imagine these positive vibes flowing out as a colored light or energy. Have them sit for a moment with their feelings, paying attention to the heart area, before opening their eyes.

Humming and Rocking

In his book *My Grandmother's Hands: Racialized Trauma and Pathways to Mending Our Hearts and Bodies*, Resmaa Menakem (2017) recommends humming, chanting, singing, and rhythmic movement to stimulate the vagus nerve. For example, the Bee Breathing method found in Chapter 6 could serve as a simple technique to engage in humming. Menakem teaches that humming from the belly as one exhales can stimulate the vagus nerve. A more comfortable alternative for students could be to hum a familiar tune—a song, a melody, a gospel tune, a lullaby—from the belly, beginning to end. Then, encourage students to stop and pay attention to their bodies. Another vagus-stimulating activity is to have students slowly rock their upper body from side to side or forward and back. You can play a soothing tune or beat and have them slow-rock to that. Students can experiment with standing versus sitting when they rock. If you want to have them practice a quicker version that doesn't require standing or space doesn't allow them to rock their bodies, an alternative Menakem recommends is to keep the body still but let the head and neck rock slowly from side to side.

Establish Social Connection

Creating a positive learning environment and ensuring students feel safe and connected in the classroom space is essential. A simple polyvagal approach, based on the idea of co-regulating one's nervous system through interaction with another, could be to design activities where students share, connect, and listen deeply to each other. Perhaps this could translate to warmly greeting students at the classroom door or simply asking, "How are you doing? Are you doing okay?" Another strategy could be to take a few minutes prior to classroom instruction and have students pair up and ask each other how they are doing or share something positive going on in their lives, a hobby, a movie or television series they like watching, etc. The idea is to foster connection.

Expressing Gratitude/Looking for the Positive

Another strategy to teach students to self-regulate is to build in small practices or daily rituals, where they look for the positive, or what Dana (S-cool, 2019) calls "glimmers" in the day. Developing a positive outlook can help us create a new platform or "set point" in the nervous system. At the end of the school day, ask students to list three things that went well (big or small)—they spent time with a friend or family member, someone smiled at them, they made the sports team, they learned something interesting. Have them sit with the feelings they experience when mentally reliving these positive moments.

Chapter 9

Relaxation and Visualization-Based Strategies for the K–12 Classroom

WHAT ARE RELAXATION AND VISUALIZATION METHODS TO REDUCE STRESS AND ANXIETY?

In this chapter, we will explore relaxation-based strategies and visualization as strategies to assist students in intentionally activating the parasympathetic nervous system (PNS) and calming the amygdala. Relaxation methods involve intentionally releasing tension from our muscles or using rhythmic sounds or movement to induce the rest and digest response. Visualization, a method long used by Olympic athletes and other top performers, requires creating mental images to produce feelings of calm and relaxation.

What Is Progressive Muscle Relaxation and How Does It Work?

A widely used technique, progressive muscle relaxation (PMR) was developed by Dr. Edmund Jacobson in the 1920s. PMR, which involves relaxing and tensing fourteen different muscle groups, was originally used to treat anxiety but expanded to address tension headaches, joint disorders, neck pain, insomnia, bipolar disorder, high blood pressure, and other disorders and ailments (Mirgain & Singles, 2016). PMR involves two steps: The first is to intentionally create tension in specific muscle groups (the concept is that in order to relax you must first experience tension or tightness). The second step requires releasing the muscle tension and noticing the feelings of relaxation. Through repetitive practice, one begins to develop awareness and differentiate between stress or tension in the muscles and the experience of complete relaxation/non-tension. PMR utilizes a neuronal "top-down" and "bottom-up" approach to achieve results (Toussaint et al., 2021). During the top-down process, practitioners focus on releasing tension in areas higher in the nervous system, including the cerebral cortex and the cerebellum while the bottom-up activity holds and releases tension in peripheral muscles that ascend to the brain through the spinal cord and brainstem.

PMR can be practiced sitting or lying down (which may not be practical for the classroom). Practitioners are advised not to overly tense or strain the muscles—just a small amount of tension will do. Another tip is to encourage synchronizing the breath with the movements or tensing (like in yoga). It may also help to experiment with different phrases to encourage relaxation, such as mentally repeating the word "relax" as you release a muscle group (Mirgain & Singles, 2016). An abridged or condensed version of PMR can be practiced, which is maybe more beneficial to the classroom, considering time constraints. Exact instructions for PMR are presented later in this chapter.

PMR's effectiveness in reducing stress and tension has been well documented through empirical research. For example, when studying thirty, first-year nursing students using the technique, researchers (Jyothimol & Lobo, 2020) noted a significant reduction in stress levels. Practicing PMR also helped reduce depression and anxiety in patients with coronary heart disease and those with cancer (Chaudhuri et al., 2020; Pradhan et al., 2020).

What Is the Relaxation Response and How Does it Work?

Another technique shown to reduce stress and anxiety is the Relaxation Response. A concept coined by cardiologist Herbert Benson in the 1970s, the Relaxation Response (RR) is a term used to describe the body's counter-point from the stress (fight or flight) response. Explained as a state of deep relaxation and reduced psychological and physiological arousal, indicators of RR entail decreased heart rate, lowered blood pressure, less muscle tension, and increased flow of blood to the brain. Benson noticed the state when conducting research on mind–body methods, including meditation. While first focusing on the stress-reduction benefits of transcendental meditation (TM), Benson claimed that similar effects could be achieved through other methods such PMS, deep breathing, prayer, and visualization. Introduced to the West in the late 1950s by Maharishi Mahesh Yogi, TM involves learning the meditation technique for four days from a certified instructor, receiving a personal mantra (sound), and paying a fee. Created by Benson, the RR technique does not require direct instruction, and one can create their own mantra.

RR has been widely used to treat a variety of medical disorders associated with stress, including headaches, hypertension, anxiety, and insomnia
(Benson et. al, 1974; Goodale et al., 1990; Jacobs et al., 1993). To elicit
RR, Benson explains that four elements are needed: (1) a quiet environment
with as few distractions as possible, (2) a mental device—a word, sound, or
phrase that is repeated, which acts as a constant stimulus and counters "mind
wandering" by bringing the distracted mind back, (3) a passive attitude or
"let it happen" attitude, and (4) a comfortable position (Benson & Klipper,
1975). Note: Exact instructions for guiding students using the RR technique
are provided later in this chapter.

How Does Progressive Muscle Relaxation and the Relaxation Response Reduce Stress and Anxiety (and Calm Our Amygdala)?

Combining muscle-tension release and diaphragmatic breathing, PMR works
by triggering the parasympathetic nervous system (PNS). The result is one
experiences the exact opposite symptoms of a stress response: slower heart
rate, lower blood pressure, etc. Muscle relaxation techniques can help dull
sympathetic nervous system (SNS) arousal. Similarly, the RR technique
works by reducing SNS activation and enhancing the PNS response. During
the RR technique, individuals' physiological measures move in the opposite
direction of the stress response: decreased oxygen consumption, carbon diox-
ide elimination, and reduced heart and respiratory rates (Benson et al., 1974).

How Are Progressive Muscle Relaxation and the Relaxation Response Methods Being Implemented in K–12 Schools?

While difficult to quantify, there has been increased interest in introducing PMR and RR, along with transcendental meditation in schools as sole
interventions or part of a larger social-emotional program. A research base
has grown around the subject, showing promising results. For instance, the
benefits of meditation with secondary students include better cognitive functioning, enhanced emotional regulation, improved well-being, fewer behavior problems, less anxiety, better sleep, and psychological changes, such as
decreased blood pressure and heart rate (e.g., Barnes et al., 2003; Beauchemin
et al., 2008; Benson et al., 1974; Bootzin & Stevens, 2005; Rosaen & Benn,
2006). While most studies examined the use of TM in schools, one found that
students practicing Benson's relaxation response for 15 minutes at the start of
health classes (which met three times per week) showed significant improvement in self-esteem and internal locus of control compared with a control

group (Benson et al., 1974). Another study involving fifth-grade Lebanese students practicing Benson's RR technique each morning before class for 10 minutes over a six-week period showed reductions in stress and anxiety levels (Day and Sadek, 1982). The intervention consisted of students sitting comfortably, relaxing their bodies, breathing out, and mentally repeating the word "one."

Regarding the use of PMR in schools, in a comprehensive review, Laypath (2001) concluded that due to the relatively small body of research in the area, it was difficult to make any strong assertions. While PMR has been generally received positively by educators and students, study findings are mixed. For example, in one study, students engaging in PMR demonstrated a significant reduction in headaches (Larson, 1990), while in another study they did not (Passchier et al., 1990). Mixed results were also found for PMR as an intervention for anxiety (Laypath, 2001).

What Is Visualization and How Does It Work?

"A therapeutic technique that has been used for centuries" (Krau, 2020, p. 473) visualization-based techniques involve using the imagination to create calming images to reduce stress and anxiety. Visualization-based methods, also referred to as guided imagery or mental rehearsal, have been empirically proven to reduce stress, anxiety, depression, and insomnia; decrease blood pressure, heart rate, and cortisol; boost feelings of calm and well-being; and strengthen coping mechanisms (e.g., Aksu et al., 2023; Beizaee et al., 2018; Chen et al., 2018). Guided imagery has also been found to enhance performance in various areas, including sports, which is why top athletes have been turning to visualization for years (Ekeocha, 2015; Martin et al., 1999; Meyers et al., 1980; Shanks & Cameron, 2000).

Visualizing consists of mentally rehearsing or "seeing" images, scenarios, or outcomes in your mind. While some people seem to be better at visualizing, it is a skill that you can develop over time with practice (Predoiu et al., 2020). Even younger children can visualize, with the ability to picture images of moving objects and change their internal representations appearing after the age of seven or eight (Rieser, Garing, & Young, 1994). Guided imagery is based on the concept that the mind and body are interconnected, and neuroscience imaging shows that the brain struggles to discriminate between an *actual* event and one rehearsed in the mind (Dijkstra & Fleming, 2023). When we vividly imagine something, since the brain encodes the strength of real or imagined stimuli in the same manner, we can experience a sort of reality distortion. In positive terms, this means we can use guided imagery to vividly see ourselves reaching goals, performing well, or in a relaxed, centered place, able to cope with life's stressors. It should also be noted that researchers have found positive results when combining visualization with physical relaxation methods, including PMR.

Guided imagery has been used successfully in medical settings for patients experiencing a variety of illnesses. In one study, fibromyalgia patients, who participated in six weeks of guided imagery, showed significant improvement in their ability to cope with the disorder (Chiaramonte et al., 2015). In a review of studies involving guided imagery and cancer patients, King (2010), noted that, in three of the five studies, patients' pain intensity decreased in experimental groups compared with control groups, who did not use imagery. Researchers using audio-recorded guided imagery with patients ages six to fifteen years old diagnosed with abdominal pain reported that the technique "was superior" to treating the condition compared to only relying on standard medical care (van Tilburg et al., 2009).

Guided imagery can be generally categorized into five types: (1) pleasant imagery of a peaceful, stress-free location, such as on a beach listening to the waves or on a favorite vacation spot; (2) physiologically focused imagery, for example, patients imagining white cells fighting cancerous cells; (3) mental rehearsal for a performance, such as giving a presentation; (4) mental reframing or visualization as a way to reinterpret one's past experience; and (5) receptive imagery or scanning the body for diagnostic or reflective purposes (see Huang et al., 2010). For the purposes of this book, we will focus on the first type, visualizing as a way to help students to relax and de-stress—in other words, using the imagination to generate positive mind–body responses (Rossman, 2010).

How Has Guided Imagery Been Used in K–12 Classrooms?

In general, research suggests that the use of guided imagery with children and teens can reduce stress, anxiety, and trauma. While researching guided imagery as an intervention within educational contexts has occurred predominately in higher education, for example, in nursing programs (Windle et al., 2021), the technique's experimentation in K–12 classrooms dates back to at least the late 1970s and 1980s (Galyean, 1981, 1982) and has continued in small doses (Kapoor et al., 2010). However, pinpointing the effectiveness of guided imagery in schools and its prevalence are difficult since such techniques are often combined with other interventions, such as mindfulness, and part of larger interventions. Visualization techniques have been explored with students for various reasons, including stress and anxiety and to enhance academic performance. In a study with sixty South Indian high school students, guided imagery techniques reduced test anxiety significantly in an experimental group (Panneerselvam & Govindharaj, 2016).

How Does Guided Imagery Reduce Stress and Anxiety?

By using the senses together, visualization techniques "produce regenerative changes in the mind and body" (Apóstolo & Kolcaba, 2009, p. 405). By removing you from the mentally stressful situation, engaging in guided imagery calms the sympathetic system. Guided imagery assists an individual in experiencing a state of psychological and physiological ease, a rest and digest response. Essentially, the mind–body system signals that the "threat" is gone and you can relax.

Relaxation and Visualization-Based Strategies for the Elementary Classroom

Progressive Muscle Relaxation (for Children)

As with other stress-reducing strategies in this book, educators want to make these relaxation and visualization activities "kid-friendly" by using certain language, tapping the imagination, and approaching it with a sense of play. There are various PMR scripts for children, such as this one (below) created by the University of Washington. When getting started, teachers may also want to play a guided video for students, such as: Guided PMR Video for Kids(SmileandLearn,2022). Here is an abridged version of PMR (adapted from the University of Washington Education Department) to use when pressed for time:

> *Today, we are going to learn to relax and let go of our stress by tightening our muscles first and then relaxing them. Please begin by taking a few deep breaths. Now:*
>
> - *Imagine your hands are like oranges. Pretend we are going "squeeze" the juice out of them. Go ahead and tighten them for five seconds, gently squeezing them (do not tighten too hard). Then, after the juice is squeezed out of your hands, completely release and relax them. Wiggle your fingers if you like.*
> - *Next, pretend you are a cat, who wants to stretch. Stretch your arms above your head, gently arching your back. Feel your back and shoulders tighten a little. Hold it for three seconds. Let's repeat a few times. Then, completely relax your arms, shoulders, and back.*
> - *Now, imagine a fly has landed on your nose. Without using your hands, pretend to get him off by scrunching up your face and nose. Move your jaw muscles (move your mouth). Again, scrunch your nose up, and hold for three seconds. Now, relax—the fly is gone!*
> - *Finally, pretend you are a tree. Your feet and legs are the trunk with roots going deep in the ground. Tighten your legs and feet for three seconds, imagine they are sinking deep into the earth. Now relax them.*

Relaxation Response for Children

Using this method, adopted from Benson's work, inform students that they are going to learn to use a sound or syllable to relax and decrease "stress" or "bad feelings" in the body. Discuss with the class how sounds, such as Lyla byes or music, can soothe us. Let them know they are going to create their own soothing sound.

1. Invite students to sit comfortably, back straight, hands resting easily in the lap.
2. Ask them to close their eyes.
3. Guide students through a brief progressive muscle relaxation, starting with tensing and relaxing the feet, then the legs, the stomach, the shoulders and neck, and finally, the face.
4. Instruct them to become aware of the breath as it comes in through the nose. On the next inhale, guide them to repeat a word, such as "one" to themselves silently. They can choose another comforting word, such as "love" or "happy."
5. Guide them to mentally repeat this word, without forcing. Tell them to repeat it gently, like they are whispering it to themselves.
6. After three to five minutes, tell them to keep their eyes closed and stretch their bodies. Give students a minute or two before emerging from the practice. If time permits, you can ask students how they feel after practicing the technique; for example, does their body feel more "relaxed"? Do they feel "calmer"?

Guided Imagery for Children

As with PMR, educators may feel more comfortable playing a guided video or having students listen to a pre-recorded audio script when introducing guided imagery. There is a plethora of guided imagery videos recorded for children. For instance, the Children's Hospital of Orange County, California, provides free resources to share with children (https://www.choc.org/programs-services/integrative-health/guided-imagery/). Here is a brief guided imagery script, adapted from the book *Meditation for Mini's* (Wildi, 2010) to get started with embedding guided imagery into the elementary classroom:

> *Invite students to sit in a comfortable position, close their eyes and take a few deep breaths. Ask them to imagine standing on a beautiful beach—either one they visited or one they create with their imagination. Then, say the following: "Feel the sand beneath your feet, between your toes. You hear the seagulls. You hear the ocean waves rolling into the shore. Can you feel the warm sun on your skin? You see a colorful seashell on the shore and pick it up. Imagine this*

is a magical shell. Whatever secrets you tell it, it listens. You can share with this shell any worries or things bothering you and it will take it away. No one else will hear! Go ahead and tell the shell what's on your mind (make sure to say this silently so classmates do not hear).

Now, the shell begins to shine a light on you, a warm glow. You feel happy, safe, and peaceful. Your whole body begins to relax. Enjoy the feelings. Remember, you can revisit this place and your magic shell anytime you want, anytime you feel upset. Now, imagine the beach gradually disappearing. Take a few deep breaths, and when ready open your eyes.

Relaxation and Visualization-Based Strategies for the Secondary Classroom

While the following strategies are essentially the same for middle and high school students, the approach, tone, and vocabulary have been adjusted to be more developmentally appropriate and provide the proper level of challenge.

Progressive Muscle Relaxation (for Teenagers)

This PMR script has been adapted from the work of Dr. James Wellborn (2016), a clinical psychologist with a focus on children and adolescents. Begin by explaining to students that you will share with them a researched-backed technique that can help them relax by systematically releasing tension in the body. Briefly discuss how they will purposefully tense each muscle group for five seconds, without straining, then completely relax it. Note that synchronizing the breath with each tensing is very important to the effectiveness of the method. Also, if students are allowed to have cell phones or laptops at the desk, make sure to ask them to turn off devices and put them out of sight, so as to not cause distraction (this is a good practice before starting any of the strategies in this book). Then, follow this script:

"Sit comfortably, close your eyes, and take a deep breath through your nose, then exhale slowly. Now, go ahead and tense your feet by curling your toes and flexing your feet. Hold for five seconds (1, 2, 3, 4 . . . 5). Release all tension in the feet. Notice how the feet feel relaxed now, how they feel different from bring tensed. Now, move your attention to your calves. Do the same thing—tense them without straining for five seconds then completely release. Next, tense the thighs and release. Move to your stomach, back, and chest. Again, notice what it feels like when this muscle group is completely relaxed. Shift to the fingers, hands, and forearms—hold for five seconds and release. Then, your biceps and triceps. Now, tense the shoulders and neck and release. Tense your cheeks, jaw, and

forehead, and count to five to yourself. Stop tensing and take a few deep breaths.
Be present with any feelings of relaxation in your entire body.

If educators would prefer to play a recording of a PMR script for students, there are many resources available on the Internet. Dartmouth College provides a website offering free recordings for PMR as well as guided imagery, mindfulness, and meditation. Visit the menu at students.dartmouth.edu/wellness-center/wellness-mindfulness/mindfulness-meditation/guided-recordings#guided.

The Relaxation Response Method for Secondary Students

When introducing the RR method, educators might briefly mention the empirical research and benefits associated with the RR method as a way to activate the parasympathetic nervous system. Explain that gently repeating a word, phrase, or motion while sitting quietly in a comfortable position can cause breathing to slow, a decrease in heart rate, etc. This experience serves as the opposite of the stress response. After learning, students can practice for ten minutes in the morning before school or after the school day to decompress. Use the following steps when inviting students to practice RR in the classroom.

1. Ask students to sit comfortably, back straight, hands resting easily in the lap. Ask them to close their eyes.
2. Guide students through a brief progressive muscle relaxation, starting with tensing and relaxing the feet, then the legs, the stomach, the shoulders and neck, and finally, the face.
3. Instruct them to become aware of the breath as it comes in through the nose. On the next inhale, guide them to repeat a word, such as "one," to themselves silently. Explain that they can also try using a phrase, such as "peace and calm" or another they create. Tell them to experiment with what works best.
4. Guide them to mentally repeat this word, without forcing. Tell them it is natural that when practicing this technique they may become distracted by thoughts or outside noise. Direct them to gently come back to their word or phrase if they become distracted.
5. After five minutes, tell them to keep their eyes closed and stretch their bodies. Give students a minute or two before "emerging" from the practice. If time permits, you can ask students how they feel after practicing the technique.

Guided Imagery for Middle and High School Students

Like the other practices in this chapter, there are many guided imagery scripts and approaches that can be used with young people. When introducing teens to guided imagery, explain that researchers have discovered, for example, that the brain cannot distinguish between what is real and what is vividly imagined, and we can use this information to "rewire" the brain to de-stress, build confidence, and improve performance. Help students understand that guided imagery can bring on relaxation and reduce stress by imagining a soothing, supportive environment and mentally removing any stressors. Emphasize that guided imagery involves using the five senses to "transport" ourselves to a place of peace, calm, and self-regulation. Also, inform students that if they cannot visualize with perfect clarity, that is okay; the technique can still work. As noted previously in this chapter, various resources exist for guided imagery on the Internet—Dartmouth College's Wellness Center offers several recorded guided imagery experiences, including a peaceful Forest Walk.

For those wanting to directly facilitate, here is a script to get started with guided imagery:

> *We are going to use guided imagery to create a calm, positive environment and let go of stress and worry. Today, we are going to take a "mini vacation" in our mind. Please close your eyes and take three deep breaths. Using your imagination, think of a peaceful place, one where you feel relaxed, calm, happy, and/or positive energy. This place can be somewhere you have visited or somewhere you would like to go. It doesn't even have to be a real place. Take a moment to imagine this place. What does it look like? What colors do you see? Is it in nature? Does it have buildings? Do you see people, animals, perhaps a river or ocean or mountains? Now, what do you hear in this place? Are people laughing, or talking? Do you hear music, or birds chirping, maybe ocean waves? What about smells? Can you smell food or flowers? Are you tasting delicious food or drinking something cool and refreshing? Finally, focus on your sense of touch. Are you holding anything? Do your feet feel the sand? Is your body enjoying water? Do you feel relaxed and stress-free? Take a moment to soak up this positive, beautiful experience. Then, when ready, take three deep breaths and slowly open your eyes.*

If time allows, you can ask students if they want to share their experiences or how they feel after the guided imagery. Have them consider their tension levels before and after the technique.

Chapter 10

Reducing Your Own
Stress as an Educator

This book has focused on ways to reduce stress in students. Of course, this can make a major difference in the classroom. But what about you? What are you doing to reduce and manage stress levels, so you can be at your best each day? Often educators, with their big hearts and attention on students, forget or neglect to follow their own stress-reduction plans and engage in mind–body practices themselves, such as the ones outlined in this book. Therefore, this chapter is dedicated to providing practical, effective ways to address personal stress levels.

EDUCATOR STRESS

As you likely know, teaching can be an extremely stressful profession. In fact, teachers have higher-than-average burnout rates compared to other professions (Kyriacou, 2015). Consequently, when teachers are stressed or burned out, that negatively impacts their behavior, which, in turn, hurts student learning and performance (Klusmann et al., 2016). Educators face high levels of stress when dealing with the expectations of students, parents, administrators, and society (Csaszar et al., 2018; Kyriacou, 2001; Lambert & McCarthy, 2006). In addition, teachers deal with difficult relationships with colleagues, administrators, and school staff and must manage student behavior (Admiraal et al., 2000; Geving, 2007). One of the main sources of teacher stress—and cause to leave the profession—is actually classroom disruptions, when students engage in disruptive behavior, interrupting instruction or disregarding school or classroom norms (Kyriacou, 2001). Stress comes with the territory as an educator; however, as I. E., Csaszar and colleagues (2018) warn:

If teachers do not possess skills to positively adapt to stress, they may experi-ence increased stress. Increased stress might lead to more negative outcomes, most notably, the experience of a pattern of emotional exhaustion progressing to burnout, decreased empathy toward others, feelings of fatigue, loss of com-passion, becoming experientially avoidant (avoiding internal thoughts, feelings, and experiences), and reduced effectiveness, which can further exacerbate the stress teachers feel. (p. 94)

Brief Overview of Teacher Stress Interventions

The good news is there has been an increase in the development of stress interventions for teachers but a general lack of empirical evidence to sup-port their effectiveness and usability (Embse et al., 2019). While there have been significant clinical advancements in treating stress and anxiety, these interventions have not necessarily been tested with teachers or in educational environments. Of the four different categories of teacher stress interven-tions—cognitive-behavioral, behavioral, mindfulness, and psychoeduca-tional or knowledge-based approaches—the treatments relying strictly on knowledge-based (solely providing information) appear to be the least effec-tive. Effective interventions are those that require teachers to make behavior changes (Embse et al., 2019).

The remainder of this chapter will outline different stress management strategies, particularly suited for educators, that can be put into place imme-diately. Like the advice given for the mind–body practices throughout this book for students, start small. Begin with trying out a stress-reduction method or approach, see how it works for you, and then when ready, add another. Continue stacking them as you build a solid approach for yourself. As we have learned, stress is inevitable, but the levels and kinds of stress are more under our control than previously thought.

Mindfulness and Meditation for Educators

As you have learned, mindfulness involves cultivating intentional, present-moment awareness. Teacher education scholars assert that mindful-ness training can help those entering the teaching profession with specific coping strategies to help them manage stress levels and build feelings of competence (Villate & Butand, 2017). In a study involving elementary school teachers, researchers (Gold et al., 2010) reported that teachers showed sig-nificant improvement in stress, anxiety, and depression-related symptoms. Likewise, R. W. Roeser and colleagues (2013) found that when teachers participated in an eight-week, after-school mindfulness training, they showed lower stress and burnout levels and greater levels of mindfulness, memory capacity, and job-related self-compassion, as opposed to a control group. The following are some mindfulness-based strategies that teachers and other educators can begin using:

Grounding Exercise

This technique relies on using the senses to bring you back to the present moment. Often, when feeling overwhelmed, we are stuck in the past or projecting into the future. To practice mindful grounding, engage in the following steps:

- Take a few breaths and bring awareness to your surroundings.
- Identify five things you can see in your environment. Just look at them without analysis.
- Become aware of four things you hear (e.g., traffic, people talking, a dog barking, your breath).
- Feel three objects in your proximity. Pay attention to their texture and shape.
- Smell two things around you. Breathe in and be aware (it is okay if you can't specifically smell anything).
- Finally bring awareness to your sense of taste (e.g., maybe some leftover coffee or something from breakfast, saliva, etc.).
- Take a breath and continue with your day.

Three-Minute Breathing Space

Taught by L. Hall (2013), this can be done anywhere and takes, as the name implies, just a few minutes. Begin by closing your eyes or gazing downward. During the first minute, ask yourself: *What are my thoughts? What are my feelings? What are my bodily sensations?* Allow answers to come easily into your awareness. During the next minute, shift awareness to how your breath flows in and out of the nostrils. Simply be aware or observe. Finally, spend the third minute widening your perspective by bringing awareness to your whole body and the space around you.

Establishing a Personal Meditation Practice

While space does not allow for a fully detailed explanation of meditation and how to cultivate a personal practice, the following tips can help you on the path.

Choose a Method

Deciding upon a meditation method can be overwhelming since there are many techniques out there. Perhaps begin with a straightforward practice, such as a mindfulness meditation that involves focusing on the breath, a loving-kindness meditation, or body awareness. There is a plethora of books, videos, and apps to get started. Don't discount movement-based meditation (as discussed in this book), such as yoga, tai chi, or qigong. Such an approach might better fit your temperament and lifestyle. To find a method that suits your needs, experiment with one for a week or so. See how your mind and body feel afterward. For example, do you feel more refreshed or more alert? As you go through your day, do you feel less reactive and more in the present moment? It can take some time to reap the benefits, and everyone progresses at a different pace.

How Long Should You Meditate?

There is no consensus on the "perfect" length of time to meditate. Generally, meditation teachers suggest starting with five to ten minutes and building up. A good session might be fifteen to twenty minutes in the morning or evening. Research shows that the biggest barrier to mediation is the time-commitment (Anderson et al., 2019). Therefore, commit to a reasonable amount of time that you can dedicate to practice, and stick to it. That might mean waking up ten minutes early or foregoing another activity, but the benefits can be worth it.

Where to Meditate?

You can really meditate anywhere (well, not driving a car or operating heavy machinery). Obviously, you want to be in a safe, relatively quiet area, where you can allow your mind to let go. It can be helpful to designate a room or corner of a room as your "meditation nook." Having a familiar space to return to each day can assist your mind in knowing it is time for meditation. Another tip is to meditate in nature whenever possible, as it can enhance your experience.

When Should I Meditate?

The best time to meditate is probably in the morning before you get too busy. Morning meditation can set a calming, positive tone for the day. Another time that might work well is in the evening, a few hours before bed. There are times when the mind—our brain wave activity—is producing alpha waves, which are slower brain waves produced by meditation or other calming activities.

Keep a Gratitude Journal

Studies show that simply reflecting on things you are grateful for (what are three blessings in my life?) can cause you to feel better about life, more positive, and connected to others (see, e.g., Emmons & McCullough, 2003; Froh et al., 2008; Lyubomirsky et al., 2005). David Chan 2011 found that when teachers kept a gratitude journal for eight weeks, they improved in life satisfaction and well-being and were less likely to experience de-personalization and alienation, which are contributing factors to burnout. Take advantage of these findings by taking a few minutes each morning or before going to bed to write down three things (e.g., events, people, situations) that you are thankful for and feel or relive those things (it's very important to feel the associated emotions).

Focus on Building Student Relationships

Research shows that student-teacher relationships have a major impact on teacher stress and burnout. "Warm" teacher-student relationships are often cited as the main reason for teachers to remain in the profession (O'Conner et al., 2008). On the other hand, negative student-teacher interactions contribute to tension, negative emotions, and discontent with work (Harmsen et al., 2018). While connecting with students and managing behaviors is extremely difficult at times, it then makes sense to focus considerable effort on increasing one's ability to relate to students, form bonds, and manage classroom behaviors. In light of the research on classroom disruptions and how it creates teacher stress, focus as much as possible on learning to manage and reduce disruptions, within your capacity. Seek out training and support in this area, as the rewards can be worth the time and effort when it comes to your stress level.

Consider Completing Formal Training

There are a number of trainings designed to teach stress-coping strategies, including ones aimed particularly at teacher stress and well-being. While this is not an exhaustive list, some of these include the Mindfulness-based Stress Reduction program, which was originally designed for medical patients but is used by people from all walks of life. There is also the Cultivating Awareness and Resilience in Education (CARE) program, which teaches cognitive-based strategies, mindfulness-based skills, and approaches for conflict resolution and behavior management. Other programs include the Stress Management and Relaxation Techniques in Education (SMART) program, an eight-week professional development course that includes mindfulness training, and the Community Approach to Learning Mindfully (CALM) program, which focuses on creating a culture of self-care and well-being in school communities.

Find Your Teacher Tribe

Another buffer against teacher stress and burnout is collaboration and building positive relationships and support circles with other educators. Research suggests that cooperation among teachers and colleague support can serve as a resource. Teachers sharing their goals, interests, and experiences can boost psychological health (Klusmann et al., 2008; Johnson and Johnson, 2003; Roeser et al., 2013). In a longitudinal study involving 2,648 teachers and spanning several years, A. Wolgast and N. Fischer (2017) found that teachers who prepared classes together, for example, designing an upcoming instructional unit, experienced higher levels of colleague support in the second year. Furthermore, teachers cooperating together on instructional planning also reported lower levels of stress than those who did not. Therefore, an action step in developing your stress-reduction plan could be identifying a colleague and asking them if they would like to plan classes together. Perhaps you could do this over coffee or during lunch once per week.

Create a Teacher Self-Care Plan

"Self-care" has become a mainstream word in society. Developing a self-care plan—an intentional series of doable actions to reduce stress and maintain wellness—has been highly recommended for educators. M. Lawler (2020) recommends the following steps to develop a self-care routine:

1. Understand that self-care is not a one-size-fits-all approach. Experiment to find what brings you joy and a sense of being centered. Use those elements to personalize your self-care routine.
2. Consider how to work these items into your daily schedule. For example, can you embed some of these actions or routines into existing routines? Start small, with a behavior or two, then you can build up and add more items as you progress.
3. Set specific, measurable goals for enacting self-care behaviors each day. For example, you might write down: "Practice mindfulness meditation for 10 minutes each morning, Monday to Friday" or "Walk around the neighborhood for 20 minutes, three days per week."
4. Create a support team to make your self-care routine sustainable. Connect with others who want to engage in similar self-care activities, for example, exercising together or also spending time in nature (this also connects well with the strategy mentioned earlier on collaborating with other teachers to reduce stress).

5. Each week, evaluate your self-care routine. Is it working? Do you feel less stressed, calmer, healthier? Are the behaviors producing positive feelings and benefits? Adjust your routine as you go. If so, continue following them. If not, experiment with a different behavior.

Other Strategies and Ideas

The following is a list of other ideas you might try for stress management compiled from various sources:

- Avoid workplace gossiping and venting sessions (Will, 2023). Complaining about students and work conditions and exchanging in negative discussions on a regular basis can impact one's mood and create stress. Instead, seek out positive, creative colleagues and engage in inspiring projects and ideas.
- Be "imperfect." Stress can become perfectionism, which teachers are prone to (Mumford, n.d.). Often, educators feel like they are not doing enough or focusing on their mistakes. Instead, turn this around and focus on what you have accomplished and your strengths. Give yourself credit!
- Create space for yourself between work and personal life. Manage your schedule so you can leave work at work and focus on your personal life when away from school (Fuhrman, 2022). While this can be difficult at times, practice shifting your focus away from work-related problems when at home. Don't carry the stress with you once you leave campus. When you give yourself off-time, you can be more "on" for students when in the classroom.

Of course, this is not an exhaustive list of teacher stress-management strategies. If this is an area of interest, you are encouraged to continue developing your knowledge and skills by consulting other resources, including those featured in the "Resource" section at the end of this book. For example, Jamie Thom's (2020) *Teacher Resilience: Managing Stress and Anxiety to Thrive in the Classroom* delves into additional actions you can take to manage stress, such as being aware of self-talk, managing conflict, and setting boundaries.

FINAL THOUGHTS ON CREATING A LESS-STRESSED CLASSROOM

This book is a synthesis of mind–body practices for the K–12 classroom. Much research and legwork has gone into providing a range of stress-reducing strategies that you can immediately share with students. This information, however, is not a recipe in the sense that if you follow everything laid out in exact order you get a perfect dish. Rather, it is more of a list of ingredients that you can experiment with to create your own dish. Classrooms are unique, representing a specific group of individuals and certain dynamic. Perhaps mindfulness-based practices work particularly well with one group of students but yoga or more movement-based activities really connect with another. This can also be said for individual students. One student may love deep breathing; another student might hate it but find calm in visualizing their safe place. What is important is to be flexible and open to innovating and noticing what works and what doesn't. Another significant factor is the idea of presenting students with a variety of practices that can help them self-regulate, an incredibly powerful skill for their lives as they grow. This book allows you to share mind–body practices that can enhance awareness and students' relationships with themselves, each other, and their world. Finally, while teacher stress was placed near the end of this book, it is perhaps the priority. As educators, we must *first* practice self-regulation and manage our own stress before we can begin to establish a calm, relatively stress-free classroom. Keep this advice in mind as you embark on the journey to embed mind–body practices in your teaching.

Author's Note

If you enjoyed this book, please take a few moments to write a review of it.
Thank you!
   Amazon: https://www.amazon.com/-/he/Steve-Haberlin/dp/147587300X

Resources

The following is a list of mind–body/stress–management resources for K–12 educators.

MINDFULNESS/MEDITATION

Mindfulness for Teachers: Simple Skills for Peace and Productivity in the Classroom by Patricia Jennings: Geared toward K–12 classrooms, this book is full of practical mindfulness-based strategies to use with students.

The Power of Now by Eckhart Tolle: A classic book on mindfulness and meditation, *The Power of Now* offers practical advice and exercises for beginners.

Mindfulness: An Eight-Week Plan for Finding Peace in a Frantic World by Mark Williams and Danny Penma: This book offers a practical and accessible introduction to mindfulness meditation.

Full Catastrophe Living: Using the Wisdom of Your Body and Mind to Face Stress, Pain, and Illness by Jon Kabat-Zinn: This book introduces the practice of mindfulness-based stress reduction (MBSR), a technique for managing stress and anxiety through meditation.

Wherever You Go, There You Are by Jon Kabat-Zinn: Zinn's book offers a practical guide to mindfulness meditation, with exercises and tips for integrating mindfulness into everyday life.

Real Happiness: The Power of Meditation by Sharon Salzberg: This book offers a practical guide to meditation, with exercises and guidance for developing a daily meditation practice.

Mindfulness in Plain English by Bhante Henepola Gunaratana: In this book, readers receive a straightforward introduction to mindfulness meditation, with practical tips and exercises for beginners.

Mindful.org: A website dedicated to mindfulness and meditation, Mindful.org offers a variety of resources for beginners, including guided meditations, articles, and podcasts.

The Free Mindfulness Project: This website provides "free access to mindfulness meditation exercises by inviting the wider mindfulness community to share their resources here."

Pocketmindfulness.com: Website started by Alfred James, father of two. Lots of user-friendly, free resources.

PROMINENT MINDFULNESS/MEDITATION TEACHERS

Jon Kabat-Zinn
Jack Kornfield
Sharon Salzberg
Joseph Goldstein
Pema Chödrön
Eckhart Tolle
Tara Brach
Kristin Neff
Mark Williams
Miles Neale

MINDFULNESS AND MEDITATION APPS

Headspace: One of the most popular mindfulness and meditation apps available, Headspace offers guided meditations for beginners and advanced practitioners alike.

Calm: Another popular meditation app, Calm offers guided meditations, sleep stories, and relaxation exercises.

Insight Timer: A free meditation app with over 100,000 guided meditations from a variety of teachers, as well as a timer for self-guided meditation.

The Mindfulness App: This app offers guided meditations for beginners, as well as tools to help you establish a daily mindfulness practice.

CENTERS FOR MINDFULNESS/MEDITATION/ CONTEMPLATIVE STUDIES

UCLA Mindful Awareness Research Center
Contemplative Studies Initiative & Concentration at Brown University
Mind-Body Wellness Program at the University of Vermont
Center for Wellness & Health Promotion at Harvard University
Center for Integrative Health & Wellness at Ohio State University

MINDFULNESS PROGRAMS

Mindfulness-Based Stress Reduction: This evidence-based program was developed by Jon Kabat-Zinn and teaches mindfulness meditation as a way to reduce stress and improve overall health and well-being.Bottom of Form

Penn Program for Mindfulness: This program "provides powerful tools for coping and personal growth. Combining modern cognitive science with ancient mindfulness techniques, the program teaches participants to change the way that they experience themselves and their world."

YOGA/MOVEMENT-BASED PRACTICES

Yoga Games for Kids: 30 Fun Activities to Encourage Mindfulness, Build Strength, and Create Calm by Lani-Rosen Gallagher: The book is full of kid-friendly yoga practices and instructions.

Good Morning Yoga: A Pose-by-Pose Wakeup Story by Mariam Gates: Highly rated, the book is just like it sounds, a children's story that features yoga poses.

Tai Chi for Kids: Move with the Animals by Stuart Alve Olson: For ages four to eight, the book teaches tai chi movements through imitating animals.

Mindfulness and Yoga in Schools: A Guide for Teachers and Practitioners by Catherine Cook-Cottone: This book synthesizes teaching mindfulness and yoga in the classroom based on research findings at the time.

YOGA-RELATED WEBSITES FOR K–12 EDUCATORS

Breath for Change: This site offers some free resources, including blogs and webinars.

School-yoga.org: This site requires a paid membership but offers some free resources.

Yoga4classroms: Provides various resources for educators, including podcasts and videos.

BREATH-WORK RESOURCES

The Belly Breath by Dr. Belisa Vranich: A storybook about a boy named Cameron who rediscovers how to breath properly to reduce anxiety.

Breathing Exercises for Kids: Thirty Exercises to Help Children Calm and Focus by Giselle

Shardlow: Provides a plethora of breathing activities for children of all ages.

Schoolbreathe.org: A United Kingdom–based breathwork for schools program. Website provides some free resources, such as guided breath-work activities and downloadable posters.

RESOURCES FOR STRESS REDUCTION FOR TEACHERS

Teacher Resilience: Managing Stress and Anxiety to Thrive in the Classroom by Jamie Thom: A highly rated book that provides practical strategies for managing teacher stress, including self-talk, setting boundaries, managing conflict, and sleep.

The Burnout Cure: Learning to Love Teaching Again by Chase Mielke: The author—a classroom teacher—provides insights into how to deal with burnout.

Teacher for America: The organization's website provides free resources for burnout.

References

Admiraal, W. F., Korthagen, F. A. J., & Wubbels, T. (2000). Effects of student teachers' coping behavior. *British Journal of Educational Psychology, 70*, 33–52.

Aksu, Ç., & Ayar, D. (2023). The effects of visualization meditation on the depression, anxiety, stress and achievement motivation levels of nursing students. *Nurse Education Today, 120*, 105618.

Albrecht, N. J., Albrecht, P. M., & Cohen, M. (2012). Mindfully teaching in the classroom: A literature review. *Australian Journal of Teacher Education, 37*(12), n12.

Alfodhly, R., Aljafari, R., Alabdullatif, M., Alghamdi, A., AlOtaibi, B., & Alarfaj, A. (2021). Mindfulness and its relationship to social skills among gifted students. *Journal of Gifted Education and Creativity, 8*(2), 33–55.

American College Health Association (2016). National college health assessment: Spring 2016 reference group executive summary. Retrieved from: http://www.achancha. org/docs/NCHAII%20SPRING%202016%20US%20 REFERENCE%20 GROUP%20EXECUTIVE%20 SUMMARY.pdf

American Psychological Association (2020). Stress in American 2020: A mental health crisis. Retrieved from: https://www.apa.org/news/press/releases/stress/2020/ sia-mental-health-crisis.pdf

American Psychological Association (2022). What's the difference between stress and anxiety? Retrieved from: https://www.apa.org/topics/stress/anxiety -difference#:~:text=People%20under%20stress%20experience%20mental ,the%20absence%20of%20a%20stressor

American Psychological Association (2023). Stress effects on the body. Retrieved from: https://www.apa.org/topics/stress/body

American Psychological Association (2023). Students experiencing stress. Retrieved from: https://www.apa.org/ed/schools/primer/stress

American Psychological Association (2023). Trauma. Retrieved from: https://www .apa.org/topics/trauma

Anderson, T., Suresh, M., & Farb, N. A. (2019). Meditation benefits and drawbacks: Empirical codebook and implications for teaching. *Journal of Cognitive Enhancement, 3*, 207–20.

Andre, C. (2019). Proper breathing brings better health. Retrieved from: https://www .scientificamerican.com/article/proper-breathing-brings-better-health/

Apóstolo, J. L. A., & Kolcaba, K. (2009). The effects of guided imagery on comfort, depression, anxiety, and stress of psychiatric inpatients with depressive disorders. *Archives of psychiatric nursing, 23*(6), 403–411.

Baer, R. A., Smith, G. T., Hopkins, J., Krietemeyer, J., & Toney, L. (2006). Using self-report assessment methods to explore facets of mindfulness. *Assessment, 13*(1), 27–45.

Bailey, P., & Bremer, F. (1938). A sensory cortical representation of the vagus nerve: With a note on the effects of low blood pressure on the cortical electrogram. *Journal of Neurophysiology, 1*(5), 405–12.

Barnes, V. A., Bauza, L. B., & Treiber, F. A. (2003). Impact of stress reduction on negative school behavior in adolescents. *Health and Quality of Life Outcomes, i(*10). Retrieved from: http//www.hqlo.com/content/1/1/10

Baron, L. J. (1998). Tai Chi practice in the elementary classroom. *Canadian Journal of Research in Early Childhood Education, 6*(4), 341–52.

Bauer, C. C., Caballero, C., Scherer, E., West, M. R., Mrazek, M. D., Phillips, D. T., . . . & Chen, Y. F., Huang, X. Y., Chien, C. H., & Cheng, J. F. (2017). The effectiveness of diaphragmatic breathing relaxation training for reducing anxiety. *Perspectives in Psychiatric Care, 53*(4), 329–336.

Beauchemin, J., Hutchins, T. L., & Patterson, F. (2008). Mindfulness meditation may lessen anxiety, promote social skills, and improve academic performance among adolescents with learning disabilities. *Complementary Health Practice Review, 13*, 34–45. doi:10.1177/1533210107311624

Beets, M. W., & Mitchell, E. (2010). Effects of yoga on stress, depression, and health-related quality of life in a nonclinical, bi-ethnic sample of adolescents: A pilot study. *Hispanic Health Care International, 8*(1), 47.

Beizaee, Y., Rejeh, N., Heravi-Karimooi, M., Tadrisi, S. D., Griffiths, P., & Vaismoradi, M. (2018). The effect of guided imagery on anxiety, depression and vital signs in patients on hemodialysis. *Complementary Therapies in Clinical Practice, 33*, 184–190.

Bellinger, D. B., DeCaro, M. S., & Ralston, P. A. (2015). Mindfulness, anxiety, and high-stakes mathematics performance in the laboratory and classroom. *Consciousness and Cognition, 37*, 123–32.

Benavides, S., & Caballero, J. (2009). Ashtaga yoga for children and adolescents for weight management and psychological well being: An uncontrolled open pilot study. *Complementary Therapies in Clinical Practices, 15*, 110–14.

Benson, H., Beary, J. F., & Carol, M. P. (1974). The relaxation response. *Psychiatry, 37*(1), 37–46.

Benson, H., & Klipper, M. Z. (1975). *The relaxation response.* New York: Morrow.

Benz, H., & Weiss, H. (1989). *To the core of your experience.* Charlottesville, VA: Luminas Press.

Berger, M. T. (2021). Situating girls of color in K–12 yoga research: Reflections and results from studying an after school yoga program for at-risk youth. In *Practicing Yoga as Resistance* (pp. 255–72). Abingdon and New York: Routledge.

Bevacqua, A., Wilson, L., & Atella, L. (n.d.). Want to relax? Try yoga. Retrieved from: https://www.nytimes.com/guides/well/yoga-stress

Biegel, G. M., Brown, K. W., Shapiro, S. L., & Schubert, C. (2009). Mindfulness-based stress reduction for the treatment of adolescent psychiatric outpatients: A randomized clinical trial. *Journal of Clinical and Consulting Psychology, 77*, 855–66. doi:10.1037/ a0016241

Blumberg, P., & Flaherty, J. A. (1985). The influence of noncognitive variables in student performance. *Academic Medicine, 60*(9), 721–23.

Bootzin, R. R., & Stevens, S. J. (2005). Adolescents, substance abuse, and the treatment of insomnia and daytime sleepiness. *Clinical Psychology Review*, 25, 629–44.

Broderick, P. C., & Metz, S. (2009). Learning to BREATHE: A pilot trial of a mindfulness curriculum for adolescents. *Advances in School Mental Health Promotion*, 2, 35–46.

Brown, R. P., & Gerbarg, P. L. (2005). Sudarshan kriya yogic breathing in the treatment of stress, anxiety, and depression: Part II—clinical applications and guidelines. *Journal of Alternative and Complementary Medicine, 11*(4), 711–17.

Brulé, D. (2017). *Just breathe: Mastering breathwork*. New York: Simon and Schuster.

Buric, I., Farias, M., Jong, J., Mee, C., & Brazil, I. A. (2017). What is the molecular signature of mind–body interventions? A systematic review of gene expression changes induced by meditation and related practices. *Frontiers in Immunology*, 670.

Butzer, B., Ebert, M., Telles, S., & Khalsa, S. B. (2015). School-based yoga programs in the United States: A survey. *Advances in Mind–Body Medicine, 29*(4), 18–26.

Cassady, J. C., & Johnson, R. E. (2002). Cognitive test anxiety and academic performance. *Contemporary Educational Psychology*, 27(2), 270–295.

Caleda, B. (2021). How to start a mindfulness program at your school. https://yogaed.com/resources/start-mindfulness-program-school/

Centeio, E. E., Whalen, L., Thomas, E., Kulik, N., & McCaughtry, N. (2017). Using yoga to reduce stress and bullying behaviors among urban youth. *Health, 9*, 409–24.

Center for Educational Improvement (2021). Schools and families working together to promote mindfulness as a community-care practice. Retrieved from: https://www.edimprovement.org/post/schools-and-families-working-together-to-promote-mindfulness-as-a-community-care-practice

Chan, David. (2011). Burnout and life satisfaction: Does gratitude intervention make a difference among Chinese school teachers in Hong Kong? *Educational Psychology (Dorchester-on-Thames), 31*(7), 809–23. https://doi.org/10.1080/01443410.2011.608525

Chavel, S. M., Westerveld, M., & Spencer, S. (2003). Long-term outcome of vagus nerve stimulation for refractory partial epilepsy. *Epilepsy & Behavior, 4*(3), 302–09.

Chen, S. F., Wang, H. H., Yang, H. Y., & Chung, U. L. (2015). Effect of relaxation with guided imagery on the physical and psychological symptoms of breast cancer patients undergoing chemotherapy. *Iranian Red Crescent Medical Journal, 17*(11).

Chiaramonte, D. R., D'Adamo, C., & Amr, S. (2015). Implementation of an integrative medicine curriculum for preventive medicine residents. *American Journal of Preventive Medicine, 49*(5), S249–S256.

Christiansen, B. (1972). *Thus speaks the body: Attempts toward a personology from the point of view of respiration and posture.* New York: Arno Press.

Church, D. (2020). *Bliss brain: The neuroscience of remodeling your brain for resilience creativity, and joy.* Carlsbad, CA: Hay House, Inc.

Church, D., Stapleton, P., & Sabot, D. (2020). Brief EcoMeditation associated with psychological improvements: A preliminary study. *Global Advances in Health and Medicine, 9,* 2164956120984142.

Clark, E. J., & Rieker, P. P. (1986). Gender differences in relationships and stress of medical and law students. *Academic Medicine, 61*(1), 32–40.

Cleveland Health Clinic (2023). Sympathetic nervous system (SNS). Retrieved from: https://my.clevelandclinic.org/health/body/23262-sympathetic-nervous -system-sns-fight-or-flight

Collins, B. (2015). *Sensory yoga for kids: Therapeutic movement for children of all abilities.* Arlington, TX: Sensory World.

Cook-Cottone, C. P. (2017). *Mindfulness and yoga in schools: A guide for teachers and practitioners.* New York: Springer Publishing Company.

Creswell, J. D., Way, B. M., Eisenberger, N. I., & Lieberman, M. D. (2007). Neural correlates of dispositional mindfulness during affect labeling. *Psychosomatic Medicine, 69*(6), 560–65.

Csaszar, I. E., Curry, J. R., & Lastrapes, R. E. (2018). Effects of loving kindness meditation on student teachers' reported levels of stress and empathy. *Teacher Education Quarterly, 45*(4), 93–116.

Day, R. C., & Sadek, S. N. (1982). The effect of Benson's relaxation response on the anxiety levels of Lebanese children under stress. *Journal of Experimental Child Psychology, 34*(2), 350–356.

Dixon, M. L., & Dweck, C. S. (2022). The amygdala and the prefrontal cortex: The co-construction of intelligent decision-making. *Psychological Review, 129*(6), 1414.

Desai, R., Tailor, A., & Bhatt, T. (2015). Effects of yoga on brain waves and structural activation: A review. *Complementary Therapies in Clinical Practice, 21*(2), 112–118.

Dijkstra, N., & Fleming, S. M. (2023). Subjective signal strength distinguishes reality from imagination. *Nature Communications, 14*(1), 1627

Doll, A., Hölzel, B. K., Bratec, S. M., Boucard, C. C., Xie, X., Wohlschläger, A. M., & Sorg, C. (2016). Mindful attention to breath regulates emotions via increased amygdala–prefrontal cortex connectivity. *Neuroimage, 134,* 305–13.

Ehmke, R., & Schuster, K. (2023). How does anxiety affect kids in school? https:// childmind.org/article/classroom-anxiety-in-children/

Ekeocha, T. C. (2015). The effects of visualization and guided imagery in sports performance. https://digital.library.txstate.edu/bitstream/handle/10877/5548/ EKEOCHATHESIS-2015.pdf?sequence=1

Elias, H., Ping, W. S., & Abdullah, M. C. (2011). Stress and academic achievement among undergraduate students in Universiti Putra Malaysia. *Procedia-Social and Behavioral Sciences, 29,* 646–655.

Embse, Ryan, S. V., Gibbs, T., & Mankin, A. (2019). Teacher stress interventions: A systematic review. *Psychology in the Schools, 56*(8), 1328–43. https://doi.org/10.1002/pits.22279

Emmons, R. A., & McCullough, M. E. (2003). Counting blessings versus burdens: An experimental investigation of gratitude and subjective well-being in daily life. *Journal of Personality and Social Psychology, 84*, 377–89.

Farhi, D. (1996). *The breathing book: Good health and vitality through essential breath work*. New York: Henry Holt and Company.

Figueroa, J., & Berwick, S. (2012). *Tai chi for kids*. North Clarendon, VT: Tuttle Publishing.

Flannery, M. E. (2018). The epidemic of anxiety among today's students. *NEA Today, 28*.

Foley, J. & DuBois, F. (1937): Quantitative studies of the vagus nerve in the cat.I. The ratio of sensory and motor studies. *J Comp Neurol 67*: 49–67.

Franco, C., Mañas, I., Cangas, A. J., & Gallego, J. (2011). Exploring the effects of a mindfulness program for students of secondary school. *International Journal of Knowledge Society Research (IJKSR), 2*(1), 14–28.

Frank, J. L., Bose, B., & Schrobenhauser-Clonan, A. (2014). Effectiveness of a school-based yoga program on adolescent mental health, stress coping strategies, and attitudes toward violence: Findings from a high-risk sample. *Journal of Applied School Psychology, 30*(1), 29–49.

Fransen, M., Nairn, L., Winstanley, J., Lam, P., & Edmonds, J. (2007). Physical activity for osteoarthritis management: A randomized controlled clinical trial evaluating hydrotherapy or Tai Chi classes. *Arthritis Care & Research, 57*(3), 407–14.

Friis, A. M., & Sollers III, J. J. (2013). Yoga improves autonomic control in males: A preliminary study into the heart of an ancient practice. *Journal of Evidence-Based Complementary & Alternative Medicine, 18*(3), 176–82.

Froh, J. J., Sefick, W. J., & Emmons, R. A. (2008). Counting blessings in early adolescents: An experimental study of gratitude and subjective well-being. *Journal of School Psychology, 46*, 213–33.

Fuhrman, R. (2022). Three ways teachers can reduce their stress levels. Retrieved from: https://www.edutopia.org/article/3-ways-teachers-can-reduce-their-stress-level/

Gabrieli, J. D. (2019). Mindfulness training reduces stress and amygdala reactivity to fearful faces in middle-school children. *Behavioral Neuroscience, 133*(6), 569.

Galyean, B. C. (1982). The use of guided imagery in elementary and secondary schools. *Imagination, Cognition and Personality, 2*(2), 145–151.

Galyean, B. C., & Krishnamurti, J. (1981). Guided imagery in education. *Journal of Humanistic Psychology, 21*(4), 57–68.

Garrison Institute. (2005). Contemplation and education: A survey of programs using contemplative techniques in K–12 educational settings: A mapping report.

George, M. S., Ward Jr., H. E., Ninan, P. T., Pollack, M., Nahas, Z., Anderson, B., . . . & Ballenger, J. C. (2008). A pilot study of vagus nerve stimulation (VNS) for treatment-resistant anxiety disorders. *Brain stimulation, 1*(2), 112–121.

George, M. S., Nahas, Z., Bohning, D. E., Kozel, F. A., Anderson, B., Chae, J. H., . . . & Mu, C. M. D. P. (2002). Vagus nerve stimulation therapy: A research update. *Neurology, 59*(6_suppl_4), S56–S61.

George, M. S., Sackeim, H. A., Rush, A. J., Marangell, L. B., Nahas, Z., Husain, M. M., . . . & Ballenger, J. C. (2000). Vagus nerve stimulation: A new tool for brain research and therapy. *Biological Psychiatry, 47*(4), 287–295.

Gethin, R. (2011). On some definitions of mindfulness. *Contemporary Buddhism, 12*(01), 263–79.

Gerszberg, C.O. (2023). Best practices for bringing mindfulness into schools. https://www.mindful.org/mindfulness-in-education/

Geving, A. M. (2007). Identifying the types of student and teacher behaviors associated with teacher stress. *Teaching and Teacher Education: An International Journal of Research and Studies, 23*, 624–40.

Gilbert, C. (2002). Interaction of psychological and emotional effects with breathing dysfunction. In L. Chaitow, D. Bradley, & C. Gilbert (Eds.), *Multidisciplinary approaches to breathing pattern disorders* (5th ed., pp. 111–30). New York: Elsevier Health Sciences.

Gold, E., Smith, A., Hopper, I., Herne, D., Tansey, G., & Hulland, C. (2010). Mindfulness-based stress reduction (MBSR) for primary school teachers. *Journal of Child and Family Studies, 19*, 184–89. doi:10.1007/210826-009-9344-0

Goleman, D. (1995). *Emotional intelligence: Why it can matter more than IQ learning*. New York: Bantam.

Gotink, R. A., Vernooij, M. W., Ikram, M. A., Niessen, W. J., Krestin, G. P., Hofman, A., . . . & Hunink, M. M. (2018). Meditation and yoga practice are associated with smaller right amygdala volume: the Rotterdam study. *Brain Imaging and Behavior, 12,* 1631–1639.

Gothe, N. P., Khan, I., Hayes, J., Erlenbach, E., & Damoiseaux, J. S. (2019). Yoga effects on brain health: A systematic review of the current literature. *Brain Plasticity, 5*(1), 105–122.

Gotink, R. A., Vernooij, M. W., Ikram, M. A., Niessen, W. J., Krestin, G. P., Hofman, A., . . . & Hunink, M. G. (2018). Meditation and yoga practice are associated with smaller right amygdala volume: the Rotterdam study. *Brain Imaging and Behavior, 12*(6), 1631–1639.

Grossman, P., & Taylor, E. W. (2007). Toward understanding respiratory sinus arrhythmia: Relations to cardiac vagal tone, evolution and biobehavioral functions. *Biological Psychology, 74*(2), 263–85.

Hagins, M., & Rundle, A. (2016). Yoga improves academic performance in urban high school students compared to physical education: A randomized controlled trial. *Mind, Brain, and Education, 10*(2), 105–116.

Hall, L. (2013). *Mindful coaching: How mindfulness can transform coaching practice*. London: Kogan Page Publishers.

Hambour, V. K., Zimmer-Gembeck, M. J., Clear, S., Rowe, S., & Avdagic, E. (2018). Emotion regulation and mindfulness in adolescents: Conceptual and empirical connection and associations with social anxiety symptoms. *Personality and Individual Differences, 134*, 7–12.

Harmsen, R., Helms-Lorenz, M., Maulana, R., & van Veen, K. (2018). The relationship between beginning teachers' stress causes, stress responses, teaching behaviour and attrition. *Teachers and Teaching, 24*(6), 626–43. https://doi.org/10.1080/13540602.2018.1465404

Harrison. L. J., Manocha, R., & Rubia, K. (2004). Sahaja yoga meditation as a family treatment for children with attention deficit-hyperactivity disorder. *Clinical Child Psychology and Psychiatry, 9*, 479–97.

Harvard Medical School (2020). Understanding the stress response. Retrieved from: https://www.health.harvard.edu/staying-healthy/understanding-the-stress-response#:~:text=Chronic%20activation%20of%20this%20survival%20mechanism%20impairs%20health&text=Muscles%20tense%20and%20beads%20of,quickly%20to%20life%2Dthreatening%20situations

Heid, M. (2017). Why tai chi is as good for you as crossfit. Retrieved from: https://time.com/4758683/tai-chi-exercise/

Hernandez-Reif, M., Field, T. M., & Thimas, E. (2001). Attention deficit hyperactivity disorder: Benefits from Tai Chi. *Journal of Bodywork and Movement Therapies, 5*(2), 120–23.

Hoge, E. A., Bui, E., Mete, M., Philip, S. R., Gabriel, C., Ward, M. J., . . . & Simon, N. M. (2020). Treatment for anxiety: Mindfulness meditation versus escitalopram (TAME): Design of a randomized, controlled non-inferiority trial. *Contemporary Clinical Trials, 91*, 105965.

Holzel, B. K., Lazar, S. W., Gard, T., Schuman-Olivier, Z., Vago, D. R., Ott, U. (2011). How does mindfulness meditation work? Proposing mechanisms of action from a conceptual and neural perspective. *Perspectives on Psychological Science, 6*, 537–59.

Huang, W., Fann, A., Zhou, L., Yang, W., Cai, C., & Yue, J. J. (2010). Tai Chi, Qi Gong, and other complementary alternative therapies for treatment of the aging spine and chronic pain. In *The comprehensive treatment of the aging spine: Minimally invasive and advanced techniques* (pp. 115–119). Elsevier.

Hyde, A. M., & Spence, J. (2013). Yoga in schools: Delivering district-wide yoga education. *Journal of Yoga Service, 1*(1), 53–59.

Idler, A. M., Mercer, S. H., Starosta, L., & Bartfai, J. M. (2017). Effects of a mindful breathing exercise during reading fluency intervention for students with attentional difficulties. *Contemporary School Psychology, 21*, 323–34.

Inagaki, T. K., & Eisenberger, N. I. (2012). Neural correlates of giving support to a loved one. *Psychosomatic medicine, 74*(1), 3–7.

Jacobs, G. (2003). *The ancestral mind: A revolutionary, scientifically validated program for reactivating the deepest part of the mind.* New York: Viking.

Jacobs, G. D., Rosenberg, P. A., Friedman, R., Matheson, J., Peavy, G. M., Domar, A. D., & Benson, H. (1993). Multifactor behavioral treatment of chronic sleep-onset insomnia using stimulus control and the relaxation response: A preliminary study. *Behavior Modification, 17*(4), 498–509.

Janakiramaiah, N., Gangadhar, B. N., Murthy, P. N. V., Harish, M. G., Subbakrishna, D. K., & Vedamurthachar, A. (2000). Antidepressant efficacy of Sudarshan Kriya

Yoga (SKY) in melancholia: A randomized comparison with electroconvulsive therapy (ECT) and imipramine. *Journal of Affective Disorders, 57*(1–3), 255–59.

Jerath, R., Crawford, M. W., Barnes, V. A., & Harden, K. (2015). Self-regulation of breathing as a primary treatment for anxiety. *Applied Psychophysiology and Biofeedback, 40*(2), 107–115.

Johnson, D. W., & Johnson, R. (2003). Training for Cooperative Group Work, (w:) West, M. A., Tjosvold, D., Smith, K. G. (red.), *International Handbook of Organizational Teamwork and Cooperative Working.* New York: John Wiley & Sons.

Joss, D., Khan, A., Lazar, S. W., & Teicher, M. H. (2021). A pilot study on amygdala volumetric changes among young adults with childhood maltreatment histories after a mindfulness intervention. *Behavioural Brain Research, 399,* 113023.

Jyothimol, P. V., & Lobo, S. M. (2020). Effectiveness of relaxation technique in reducing stress among nursing students. *Int J Nurs Health Res, 2*(1), 54–56.

Kabat-Zinn, J. (2003). Mindfulness-based interventions in context: Past, present, and future. *Clinical Psychology, 10,* 2.

Kapoor, V. G., Bray, M. A., & Kehle, T. J. (2010). School-based intervention: Relaxation and guided imagery for students with asthma and anxiety disorder. *Canadian Journal of School Psychology, 25*(4), 311–327.

Kauts, A., & Sharma, N. (2009). Effect of yoga on academic performance in relation to stress. *International Journal of Yoga, 2*(1), 39.

Keller, A., Litzelman, K., Wisk, L. E., Maddox, T., Cheng, E. R., Creswell, P. D., & Witt, W. P. (2012). Does the perception that stress affects health matter? The association with health and mortality. *Health Psychology, 31*(5), 677.

King, D., Sandhu, M., Henderson, S., & Ritchie, S. M. (2018). Managing emotions: Outcomes of a breathing intervention in year 10 science. In *Eventful Learning* (pp. 193–216). Leiden, Netherlands: Brill Sense.

King, J. V. (1988). A holistic technique to lower anxiety: Relaxation with guided imagery. *Journal of Holistic Nursing, 6*(1), 16–20.

Klusmann, U., Kunter, M., Trautwein, U., Lüdtke, O., & Baumert, J. (2008). Teachers' occupational well-being and quality of instruction: The important role of self-regulatory patterns. *Journal of Educational Psychology, 100*(3), 702.

Klusmann, U., Richter, D., & Lüdtke, O. (2016). Teachers' emotional exhaustion is negatively related to students' achievement: Evidence from a large-scale assessment study. *Journal of Educational Psychology, 108*(8), 1193.

Kok, B. E., Coffey, K. A., Cohn, M. A., Catalino, L. I., Vacharkulksemsuk, T., Algoe, S. B., . . . & Fredrickson, B. L. (2013). How positive emotions build physical health: Perceived positive social connections account for the upward spiral between positive emotions and vagal tone. *Psychological Science, 24*(7), 1123–32.

Kral, T. R., Schuyler, B. S., Mumford, J. A., Rosenkranz, M. A., Lutz, A., & Davidson, R. J. (2018). Impact of short- and long-term mindfulness meditation training on amygdala reactivity to emotional stimuli. *NeuroImage, 181,* 301–313.

Krau, S. D. (2020). The multiple uses of guided imagery. *Nursing Clinics, 55*(4), 467–474.

Kutner, Nancy G., Barnhart, Huiman, Wolf, Steven L., McNeely, Elizabeth, & Tingsen Xu. (1997). "Self-report benefits of Tai Chi practice by older adults." *Journals of Gerontology Series B: Psychological Sciences and Social Sciences, 52*(5), P242–46.

Kulkarni, M. (2014). Amygdala: A beast to tame. Retrieved from: https://nopr.niscpr. res.in/bitstream/123456789/30030/1/SR%2051(12)%2038–40.pdf

Kyriacou, C. (2001). Teacher stress: Directions for future research. *Educational Review, 53*(1), 27–35. doi:10.1080/00131910120033628

Kyriacou, C. (2015). Teacher stress and burnout: Methodological perspectives. *International Encyclopedia of the Social & Behavioral Sciences.* 10.1016/B978-0-08-097086-8.92087-7.

Lagopoulos, J., Xu, J., Rasmussen, I., Vik, A., Malhi, G. S., Eliassen, C. F., . . . & Ellingsen, Ø. (2009). Increased theta and alpha EEG activity during nondirective meditation. *Journal of Alternative and Complementary Medicine, 15*(11), 1187–92.

Lambert, R. G., & McCarthy, C. (Eds.). (2006). *Understanding teacher stress in an age of accountability.* Charlotte, NC: Information Age.

Larrivee, B. (2012). *Cultivating teacher renewal: Guarding against stress and burnout.* Lanham, MD: Rowman & Littlefield.

Larson, H. A., El Ramahi, M. K., Conn, S. R., Estes, L. A., & Ghibellini, A. B. (2010). Reducing test anxiety among third grade students through the implementation of relaxation techniques. *Journal of School Counseling, 8*(19), n19.

Larson, H. A., Yoder, A. M., Brucker, S., Lee, J., Washburn, F., Perdieu, D., . . . & Rose, J. R. (2011). Effects of relaxation and deep-breathing on high school students: ACT prep. *Journal of Counseling in Illinois, 16.*

Larsson, B., Melin, L., & Doberl, A. (1990). Recurrent tension headache in adolescents 54 treated with self-help relaxation training and a muscle relaxant drug. *Headache, 30,* 665–671.

Lawler, M. (2020, April 6). How to start a self-care routine you'll follow: Everyday health. Retrieved from: https://www.everydayhealth.com/self-care/start-a-self-care -routine/

Laypath, C. (2001). *A review of progressive muscle relaxation interventions used with school-aged children and adolescents.* Retrieved from: https://digitalcommons.usu. edu/cgi/viewcontent.cgi?article=2009&context=gradreports

Lazar, S. W., Kerr, C. E., Wasserman, R. H., Gray, J. R., Greve, D. N., Treadway, M. T., . . . & Fischl, B. (2005). Meditation experience is associated with increased cortical thickness. *Neuroreport, 16*(17), 1893.

Lee, J., Semple, R. J., Rosa, D., & Miller, L. (2008). Mindfulness-based cognitive therapy for children: Results of a pilot study. *Journal of Cognitive Psychotherapy, 22*(1), 15–28. doi: http://dx.doi.org/10.1891/0889.8391.22.1.15

Li, F., Harmer, P., McAuley, E., Fisher, K. J., Duncan, T. E., & Duncan, S. C. (2001). Tai Chi, self-efficacy, and physical function in the elderly. *Prevention Science, 2,* 229–39.

Lim, S. A., & Cheong, K. J. (2015). Regular yoga practice improves antioxidant status, immune function, and stress hormone releases in young healthy people: A randomized, double-blind, controlled pilot study. *Journal of Alternative and Complementary Medicine, 21*(9), 530–38.

Lin, H. C., Lin, H. P., Yu, H. H., Wang, L. C., Lee, J. H., Lin, Y. T., . . . & Chiang, B. L. (2017). Tai-Chi-Chuan exercise improves pulmonary function and decreases exhaled nitric oxide level in both asthmatic and nonasthmatic children and improves quality of life in children with asthma. *Evidence-Based Complementary and Alternative Medicine: eCAM*, 6287642. https://doi.org/10.1155/2017/6287642

Linn, B. S., & Zeppa, R. (1984). Stress in junior medical students: relationship to personality and performance. *Academic Medicine, 59*(1), 7–12.

Long, C. (2021). How the parasympathetic nervous system can lower stress. Retrieved from: https://www.hss.edu/article_parasympathetic-nervous-system.asp

Lyubomirsky, S., Sheldon, K. M., & Schkade, D. (2005). Pursuing happiness: The architecture of sustainable change. *Review of General Psychology, 9*, 111–31.

Ma, X., Yue, Z. Q., Gong, Z. Q., Zhang, H., Duan, N. Y., Shi, Y. T., Wei, G. X., & Li, Y. F. (2017). The effect of diaphragmatic breathing on attention, negative affect and stress in healthy adults. *Frontiers in Psychology, 8*, 874. https://doi.org/10.3389/fpsyg.2017.00874

Maddalozzo, G. F., & Snow, C. M. (2000). High intensity resistance training: Effects on bone in older men and women. *Calcified Tissue International, 66*, 399–404.

Martin, K. A., Moritz, S. E., & Hall, C. R. (1999). Imagery use in sport: A literature review and applied model. *The Sport Psychologist, 13*(3), 245–268. https://doi.org/10.1123/tsp.13.3.245

McGonigal, K. (2015). *The upside of stress: Why stress is good for you, and how to get good at it.* New York: Penguin.

Medline Plus (2023). Stress and your health. Retrieved from: https://medlineplus.gov/ency/article/003211.htm

Meyers, A. W., & Schleser, R. (1980). A cognitive behavioral intervention for improving basketball performance. *Journal of Sport and Exercise Psychology, 2*(1), 69–73. https://doi.org/10.1123/jsp.2.1.69

Milkie, M. A., & Warner, C. H. (2011). Classroom learning environments and the mental health of first grade children. *Journal of Health and Social Behavior, 52*(1), 4–22.

Mind and Life Education Research Network (MLERN). J. Davidson, R., Dunne, J., Eccles, J. S., Engle, A., Greenberg, M., . . . & Vago, D. (2012). Contemplative practices and mental training: Prospects for American education. *Child Development Perspectives, 6*(2), 146–53.

Mirgain, S. & Singles, J. (2016). Progressive muscle relaxation. Retrieved from: https://www.va.gov/WHOLEHEALTHLIBRARY/tools/progressive-muscle-relaxation.asp

Mockford, M., & Caulton, J. M. (2008). Systematic review of progressive strength training in children and adolescents with cerebral palsy who are ambulatory. *Pediatric Physical Therapy, 20*(4), 318–33.

Mumford, C. (n.d.). 9 Stress management techniques every teacher needs to know. Retrieved from: https://www.wgu.edu/heyteach/article/9-stress-management-strategies-every-teacher-needs-know1612.html

Naik, G. S., Gaur, G. S., & Pal, G. K. (2018). Effect of modified slow breathing exercise on perceived stress and basal cardiovascular parameters. *International Journal of Yoga*, *11*(1), 53–58.

National Alliance on Mental Illness (2017). Anxiety disorders. https://www.nami.org/About-Mental-Illness/Mental-Health-Conditions/Anxiety-Disorders

National Center for Complementary and Integrative Health (2013). Yoga. https://files.nccih.nih.gov/s3fs-public/Yoga_for_Health_12-01-2015.pdf#:~:text=Other%20studies%20also%20suggest%20that%20practicing%20yoga%20%28as,and%20improve%20overall%20physical%20fitness%2C%20strength%2C%20and%20flexibility

National Library of Medicine (2016). How does the nervous system work? Retrieved from: https://www.ncbi.nlm.nih.gov/books/NBK279390/#:~:text=The%20sympathetic%20and%20parasympathetic%20nervous,more%20easily%2C%20and%20inhibits%20digestion

Neale, M. (2017). In Loizzo, J. E., Neale, M. E., & Wolf, E. J. (2017). *Advances in contemplative psychotherapy: Accelerating healing and transformation.* New York: Routledge/Taylor & Francis Group.

Neuhuber, W. L., & Berthoud, H. R. (2022). Functional anatomy of the vagus system: How does the polyvagal theory comply? *Biological Psychology*, 108425.

Norelli, S. K., Long, A., & Krepps, J. M. (2020). Relaxation techniques. In *StatPearls [Internet].* StatPearls Publishing.

O'Connor, K. E. (2008). "You choose to care": Teachers, emotions and professional identity. *Teaching and Teacher Education*, *24*(1), 117–26.

Pagnoni, G., & Cekic, M. (2007). Age effects on gray matter volume and attentional performance in Zen meditation. *Neurobiology of Aging*, *28*(10), 1623–27.

Panneerselvam, S., & Govindharaj, P. (2016). Effectiveness of guided imagery in reducing examination anxiety among secondary school students in south India. *Int J Ind Psych*, *3*, 54–61.

Passchier, J., Van den Bree, M. B. M., Emmen, H. H., Osterhaus, S. O. L., Orlebeke, J. F., & Vergage, F. (1990). Relaxation training in school classes does not reduce headache complaints. *Headache, 30*, 660–664.

Patterson, J. (2020). *The power of breathwork: Simple practices to promote wellbeing.* Beverly, MA: Fair Winds Press.

Paul, G., Elam, B., & Verhulst, S. J. (2007). A longitudinal study of students' perceptions of using deep breathing meditation to reduce testing stresses. *Teaching and learning in medicine*, *19*(3), 287–292.

Peck, H. L., Kehle, T. J., Bray, M. A., & Theodore, L. A. (2005). Yoga as an intervention for children with attention problems. *School Psychology Review*, *34*(3), 415–24.

Pile, V., Williamson, G., Saunders, A., Holmes, E. A., & Lau, J. Y. (2021). Harnessing emotional mental imagery to reduce anxiety and depression in young people: An integrative review of progress and promise. *The Lancet Psychiatry*, *8*(9), 836–852.

Pittman, C. M., & Karle, E. M. (2015). *Rewire your anxious brain: How to use the neuroscience of fear to end anxiety, panic, and worry.* Oakland, CA: New Harbinger Publications.

Pradhan, J., Pradhan, R., Samantaray, K., & Pahantasingh, S. (2020). Progressive muscle relaxation therapy on anxiety among hospitalized cancer patients. *European Journal of* Molecular & Clinical Medicine, 7(8), 1485–1488.

Predoiu, R., Predoiu, A., Mitrache, G., Firansecu, M., Cosma, G., G., & Buchroiu, R. A. (2020). Visualization techniques in sport-the mental roadmap for success. *Discobolul-Physical Education, Sport & Kinetotherapy Journal, 59(3).*

Redfering, D, L., & Bowman. M. J. (1981). Effect of a meditative yoga relaxation exercise on non-attending behaviors of behaviorally disturbed children. *Clinical Child Psychology, 10*, 126–27.

Reschly, A. L., Huebner, E. S., Appleton, J. J., & Antaramian, S. (2008). Engagement as flourishing: The contribution of positive emotions and coping to adolescents' engagement at school and with learning. *Psychology in the Schools*, 455, 419–31. https://doi.org/10.1002/pits.20306

Rieser, J. J., Garing, A. E., & Young M. F. (1994). Imagery, action, and young children's spatial orientation: It's not being there that counts, it's what one has in mind. *Child Development, 65*(5), 1262–1278. doi.org/10.1111/j.1467–8624.1994.tb00816.x

Roeser, R. W., Schonert-Reichl, K. A., Jha, A., Cullen, M., Wallace, L., Wilensky, R., . . . Harrison, J. (2013). Mindfulness training and reductions in teacher stress and burnout: Results from two randomized, waitlist-control field trials. *Journal of Educational Psychology, 105*, 787–804. doi:10.1037/a0032093

Rosaen, C, & Benn, R. (2006). The experience of Transcendental Meditation in middle school students: *A Qualitative Report. Explore, 2*, 422–424.

Rosenberg, J., Rand, M., & Asay, D. (1985). *Body, self and soul and sustaining integration.* Atlanta, GA: Humanics Limited.

Rosenberg, S. (2017). *Accessing the healing power of the vagus nerve: Self-help exercises for anxiety, depression, trauma, and autism.* North Atlantic Books.

Rossman, M. L. (2010). *Guided imagery for self-healing: An essential resource for anyone seeking wellness.* HJ Kramer.

Rush, A. J., George, M. S., Sackeim, H. A., Marangell, L. B., Husain, M. M., Giller, C., . . . & Goodman, R. (2000). Vagus nerve stimulation (VNS) for treatment-resistant depressions: A multicenter study. *Biological Psychiatry, 47*(4), 276–86.

Rushton, A. (2004). *What You Need to Know: Stress.* Farnham: Wellhouse.

Sackeim, H. A., Rush, A. J., George, M. S., Marangell, L. B., Husain, M. M., Nahas, Z., . . . & Goodman, R. R. (2001). Vagus nerve stimulation (VNS™) for treatment-resistant depression: Efficacy, side effects, and predictors of outcome. *Neuropsychopharmacology, 25*(5), 713–28.

Sahin, S., & Tuna, R. (2022). The effect of anxiety on thriving levels of university students during the COVID-19 pandemic. *Collegian (Royal College of Nursing, Australia), 29*(3), 263–270.

Satin, J. R., Linden, W., & Millman, R. D. (2014). Yoga and psychophysiological determinants of cardiovascular health: Comparing yoga practitioners, runners, and sedentary individuals. *Annals of Behavioral Medicine, 47*(2), 231–41.

Schwabe, L., & Wolf, O. T. (2010). Learning under stress impairs memory formation. *Neurobiology of Learning and Memory, 93*(2), 183–188.

Schmidt, J. E., Carlson, C. R., Usery, A. R., & Quevedo, A. S. (2009). Effects of tongue position on mandibular muscle activity and heart rate function. *Oral Surgery, Oral Medicine, Oral Pathology, Oral Radiology, and Endodontology, 108*(6), 881–88.

Schonert-Reichl, K. A., & Lawlor, M. S. (2010). The effects of a mindfulness-based education program on pre-and early adolescents' well-being and social and emotional competence. *Mindfulness, 1*(3), 137–51.

S'cool Moves (2019). *The polyvagal theory with Deb Dana* [video]. YouTube. https://www.youtube.com/watch?v=81ukR155DR4&t=303s

Seery, M. D., Holman, E. A., & Silver, R. C. (2010). Whatever does not kill us: Cumulative lifetime adversity, vulnerability, and resilience. *Journal of Personality and Social Psychology, 99*(6), 1025.

Selye, H. (1976). *Stress without distress.* New York: Springer US.

Semple, R. J., Droutman, V., & Reid, B. A. (2017). Mindfulness goes to school: Things learned (so far) from research and real-world experiences. *Psychology in the Schools, 54*(1), 29–52. https://doi.org/10.1002/pits.21981

Semple, R. J., Lee, J., Rosa, D., & Miller, L. F. (2010). A randomized trial of mindfulness-based cognitive therapy for children: Promoting mindful attention to enhance social-emotional resiliency in children. *Journal of Child and Family Studies, 19*, 218–29.

Seo, D. Y., Lee, S., Figueroa, A., Kim, H. K., Baek, Y. H., Kwak, Y. S., . . . Han, J. (2012). Yoga training improves metabolic parameters in obese boys. *Korean Journal Physiology Pharmacology, 16*, 175–80.

Seppälä, E. M., Nitschke, J. B., Tudorascu, D. L., Hayes, A., Goldstein, M. R., Nguyen, D. T., . . . & Davidson, R. J. (2014). Breathing-based meditation decreases posttraumatic stress disorder symptoms in US Military veterans: A randomized controlled longitudinal study. *Journal of traumatic stress, 27*(4), 397–405.

Shanks, D. R., & Cameron, A. (2000). The effect of mental practice on performance in a sequential reaction time task. *Journal of Motor Behavior, 32*(3), 305–313. https://doi.org/10.1080/00222890009601381

Shaw-Metz, J. L. (2023). Coming up for air: Breathwork practice for stress management in the healthcare setting. *Journal of Interprofessional Education & Practice, 30*, 100594.

Smalley, S. L., & Winston, D. (2010). *Fully present: The science, art, and practice of mindfulness.* Boston: Da Capo Lifelong Books.

Smile and Learn (2022, November 1). *Progressive muscle relaxation for kids, body, guided session, episode 2* [Video]. YouTube. https://www.youtube.com/watch?v=w4gJuAyPxUk

Struthers, C. W., Perry, R. P., & Menec, V. H. (2000). An examination of the relationship among academic stress, coping, motivation, and performance in college. *Research in Higher Education, 41*, 581–592.

Sundram, B. M., Dahlui, M., & Chinna, K. (2014). "Taking my breath away by keeping stress at bay": An employee assistance program in the automotive assembly plant. *Iranian Journal of Public Health, 43*(3), 263.

Taren, A. A., Gianaros, P. J., Greco, C. M., Lindsay, E. K., Fairgrieve, A., Brown, K. W., . . . & Creswell, J. D. (2015). Mindfulness meditation training alters stress-related amygdala resting state functional connectivity: A randomized controlled trial. *Social cognitive and affective neuroscience, 10*(12), 1758–1768.

Thierry, K. L., Bryant, H. L., Nobles, S. S., & Norris, K. S. (2016). Two-year impact of a mindfulness-based program on preschoolers' self-regulation and academic performance. *Early Education and Development, 27*(6), 805–21.

Toussaint, L., Nguyen, Q. A., Roettger, C., Dixon, K., Offenbächer, M., Kohls, N., . . . & Sirois, F. (2021). Effectiveness of progressive muscle relaxation, deep breathing, and guided imagery in promoting psychological and physiological states of relaxation. *Evidence-Based Complementary and Alternative Medicine, 2021.*

Treves, I. N., Olson, H. A., Ozernov-Palchik, O., Li, C. E., Wang, K. L., Arechiga, X. M., . . . & Gabrieli, J. D. (2023). At-home use of app-based mindfulness for children: A randomized active-controlled trial. *Mindfulness, 14*, 2728–44. https://doi.org/10.1007/s12671-023-02231-3

Tyagi, A., & Cohen, M. (2016). Yoga and heart rate variability: A comprehensive review of the literature. *International Journal of Yoga, 9*(2), 97–113. https://doi.org/10.4103/0973-6131.183712

Tymofiyeva, O., Henje, E., Yuan, J. P., Huang, C. Y., Connolly, C. G., Ho, T. C., . . . & Xu, D. (2021). Reduced anxiety and changes in amygdala network properties in adolescents with training for awareness, resilience, and action (TARA). *NeuroImage: Clinical, 29*, 102521.

University of California–Irvine. Short-term stress can affect learning and memory. ScienceDaily, March 13, 2008. www.sciencedaily.com/releases/2008/03/080311182434.htm

University of Minnesota (2023). What are mind-body practices? Retrieved from: https://www.takingcharge.csh.umn.edu/survivorship/what-are-mind-body-practices

University of Oregon (n.d.). Types of stress: Positive, tolerable, and toxic stress. Retrieved from: https://center.uoregon.edu/StartingStrong/uploads/STARTINGSTRONG2016/HANDOUTS/KEY_49962/TypesofStress.pdf

University of Toledo (2023). Deep breathing and relaxation. Retrieved from: https://www.utoledo.edu/studentaffairs/counseling/anxietytoolbox/breathingandrelaxation.html#:~:text=Deep%20breathing%20and%20relaxation%20activate,oxygen%20to%20the%20thinking%20brain

van Tilburg, M. A., Chitkara, D. K., Palsson, O. S., Turner, M., Blois-Martin, N., Ulshen, M., & Whitehead, W. E. (2009). Audio-recorded guided imagery treatment reduces functional abdominal pain in children: A pilot study. *Pediatrics, 124*(5), e890–e897.

Vestergaard-Poulsen, P., van Beek, M., Skewes, J., Bjarkam, C. R., Stubberup, M., Bertelsen, J., & Roepstorff, A. (2009). Long-term meditation is associated with increased gray matter density in the brain stem. *Neuroreport, 20*(2), 170–74.

Villate, V. M., & Butand, G. L. (2017). Cultivating mindful teachers: Using a mindfulness-based teaching approach with student teachers. In Dorman, E. H., Byrnes, K., & Dalton, J. E. (Eds.), *Impacting teaching and learning: Contemplative practices, pedagogy, and research in education,* 17–29. Lanham, MD: Rowman & Littlefield.

Wall, R. (2005). Tai chi and mindfulness-based stress reduction in a Boston public middle school. *Journal of Pediatric Health Care, 19*(4), 230–37.

Wellborn, J. (2016). Stress Management for Teens series (blog posts). https://drjames-wellborn.com/tag/stress-management/

Wemm, S., Koone, T., Blough, E. R., Mewaldt, S., & Bardi, M. (2010). The role of DHEA in relation to problem solving and academic performance. *Biological Psychology, 85*(1), 53–61.

Wildi, D. (2010). *Meditation for mini's: Relaxing stories to calm little minds.* Null.

Will, M. (2003). Teacher stress: 6 coping strategies. https://www.edweek.org/teaching-learning/teacher-stress-6-coping-strategies/2023/05

Willis, J. (2006). *Classroom-based strategies to ignite student learning: Insights from a neurologist and classroom teacher.* ASCD.

Windle, S., Berger, S., & Kim, J. E. E. (2021). Teaching guided imagery and relaxation techniques in undergraduate nursing education. *Journal of Holistic Nursing, 39*(2), 199–206.

Wilson, D. E. (2023). *The polyvagal path to joyful learning: Transforming classrooms one nervous system at a time.* New York: W.W. Norton & Company.

Wolgast, A., & Fischer, N. (2017). You are not alone: Colleague support and goal-oriented cooperation as resources to reduce teachers' stress. *Social Psychology of Education, 20*, 97–114.

YouthTruth (2022). *Insights from the student experience, part I.* Retrieved from: https://youthtruth.org/resources/insights-from-the-student-experience-part-i-emotional-mental-health/

Young, D. R., Appel, L. J., Jee, S., & Miller III, E. R. (1999). The effects of aerobic exercise and T'ai Chi on blood pressure in older people: Results of a randomized trial. *Journal of the American Geriatrics Society, 47*(3), 277–84.

Yuliana, Y. (2021). Amygdala changes through breathing exercise in coping with the COVID-19 Pandemic. *International Journal on Research in STEM Education, 3*(1), 07–16. https://www.mentalhealth.org.uk/explore-mental-health/a-z-topics/stress

Yu, Y., & Wang, Y. (2023). Invasive and non-invasive vagal nerve stimulation for the brain. *Frontiers in Neurology, 14*, 1269851.

About the Author

Steve Haberlin, PhD, is an assistant professor of curriculum and instruction in the College of Community Innovation & Education at the University of Central Florida. He is the author of *Meditation in the College Classroom: A Pedagogical Tool to Help Students De-Stress, Focus, and Connect* and *Awakening to Educational-Supervision: A Mindfulness-Based Approach to Coaching and Supporting Teachers.*

www.ingramcontent.com/pod-product-compliance
Lightning Source LLC
Chambersburg PA
CBHW020357270326

41926CB00007B/468